PUTT

LIKE A

PRO

FOREWORD BY JOHN ANDRISANI

PUTT
LIKE A
PRO

BRIAN LAKE

MASTER THE GROUND GAME
STROKE THAT'S RIGHT FOR YOU

New York Chicago San Francisco Lisbon London Madrid Mexico City
Milan New Delhi San Juan Seoul Singapore Sydney Toronto

The McGraw-Hill Companies

Library of Congress Cataloging-in-Publication Data

Lake, Brian.
 Putt like a pro : master the ground game stroke that's right for you / Brian Lake.
  p. cm.
 ISBN-13: 978-0-07-150822-3 (alk. paper)
 ISBN-10: 0-07-150822-8 (alk. paper)
  1. Putting (Golf)—Handbooks, manuals, etc. 2. Putting (Golf)—Psychological
aspects. I. Title.

 GV979.P8L34   2008
 796.352'35—dc22   2007033175

1 2 3 4 5 6 7 8 9 10 11 12 13 14 15 16 17 18 19 20 21 DOC/DOC 0 9 8

ISBN 978-0-07-150822-3
MHID   0-07-150822-8

Photograph 7.1 by Bruce Wooster; 8.1, 8.2, 8.3, 8.4, 8.7, 9.8, 9.11 by Brian Lake, Sr.
All others by Yasuhiro "J.J." Tanabe.
Interior design by DesignForBooks.com

McGraw-Hill books are available at special quantity discounts to use as premiums and
sales promotions or for use in corporate training programs. To contact a representative,
please visit the Contact Us pages at www.mhprofessional.com.

This book is printed on acid-free paper.

I dedicate this book to my lovely wife, Kami, and my two beautiful girls, Olivia and Averi. Without their love, support, and patience, I would have been unable to create this unique book on putting.

CONTENTS

FOREWORD

Putting involves the shortest swing in all of golf and requires the least degree of muscular strength and coordination. Yet the seemingly ultrasimple act of stroking a 1.68-inch diameter ball across a smooth green surface into a 4.25-inch diameter hole causes professional and amateur golfers the highest degree of frustration during a round of eighteen holes.

The putter is the golfer's most important scoring club. In fact, good putting is a chief reason why Tiger Woods has won more than fifty golf tournaments around the world, highlighted by twelve major championship victories.

In contrast, the chief reason America's team lost the 2006 Ryder Cup is because its players failed to sink par, birdie, and eagle putts, while opponents from Great Britain and Europe holed out from short and long range on the greens, just as they had done in recent previous Ryder Cup matches.

On the amateur front, the handicaps of country club golfers around the United States are actually rising, owing largely to poor putting scores. This is an astonishing fact when you consider that becoming a good putter, unlike a good swinger of a golf club, requires very little athletic ability.

Putting, unquestionably, constitutes the nucleus of the short game and is the department of golf that accounts for the highest percentage of a player's golf score over eighteen holes. However, due greatly to technical misinformation presented in golf magazines and books, on CDs, and even by some instructors appearing on the Golf Channel, recreational players admit to feeling a stronger sense of confusion and higher degree of pressure on the greens than on the tee swinging a driver or on the fairway hitting an iron shot.

On good putting days, golfers feel like the ball can be willed into the cup. Consequently, players are so full of confidence that they can let out the shaft on tee shots and attack the flag when hitting approaches into greens. In short, golfers who feels good about the putter can afford to play with a fearless go-for-broke attitude, knowing that even if drives miss the fairways or approach shots hit into greens fly off-line into the rough, bunkers, or heavy fringe grass, the putter will ultimately be the club in their bag that will bail them out and help them salvage par or, at worst, bogey. On bad putting days, golfers feel such pressure to keep tee shots in play and hit approach shots stiff to the hole that they frequently steer the club during the swing and end up hitting everything but fairways and greens. Putting has long been regarded as the most mysterious, most exacting department of the game, one that can bring the golfer great satisfaction or great frustration during a round.

If you mishit a tee shot and the ball lands in an on-course trouble area, you can still hit your approach onto the green. There are really no second chances on the green, especially from short range. Furthermore, when you fail to hole a couple "knee-knocker" putts in a row, you become more and more tentative. It's during these skill lapse periods that you, like your fellow golfers, become so frazzled that you start employing a nervous type of a yip stroke. All of a sudden, you start hitting poor mid-range and long putts, and before you know it, you are in a putting slump.

At this stage in a golfer's life, he or she searches for answers. Some golfers opt to buy a new putter. The problem is that average club players simply purchase one of the hottest models on the market, neglecting to get advice from their local golf pro about such custom-fit variables as putter lie, putter loft, and putter length. Other golfers that struggle on the greens, particularly high-handicap players, opt to switch from a personalized, self-made stroke to a straight-back straight-through putting stroke (advocated by putting guru Dave Pelz) or an inside-square-inside method (advocated by popular short-game instructor Stan Utley).

The irony regarding the golfer's search for a putting fix, according to this book's author, Brian Lake, is that if the golfer is not properly fitted for a putter, he or she will not be able to employ either of the two aforementioned traditional strokes to the best of his or her ability, and, moreover, either of these strokes may not even be right for the player.

In *Putt like a Pro*, Lake makes several points crystal clear. One of his points is that the variety of styles employed by great putters on the PGA Tour, LPGA Tour, Champions Tour, and Nationwide Tour is proof that putting is by far the most idiosyncratic part of the game of golf.

Top tour professionals putt with different types of putters, yet all are custom fit. Golf's greatest putters each choose to play with a specific type of golf ball—one suited to what they like to feel when bringing the putter face into the ball or the sound (for example, a click) they like to hear at impact. The setup, back-stroke, and down-stroke positions that proficient putters rely on to purposely roll a golf ball with a golf club over a specific distance along a selected path (or simply "roll the rock," as Tiger Woods says) vary quite noticeably. Regardless of the wide-ranging putting techniques employed by pros and leading amateur golfers, a few fundamentals always apply. These areas are the focal points of *Putt like a Pro*. As you will see when reading this book, Lake separates fact from fiction regarding the true common denominator fundamentals employed by today's top putters and presents plenty of information and advice about all of the most orthodox and unorthodox putting strokes, enabling you to intelligently choose the most suitable putting stroke from the eight he breaks down and explains. The putting methods covered by Lake include:

► Traditional straight-back straight-through stroke
► Traditional inside-square-inside stroke
► Claw grip stroke

- ► Belly putter stroke
- ► Stand-up stroke
- ► Cross-handed grip stroke
- ► Sidesaddle stroke
- ► Split-hand stroke

Good luck in your quest to become the world's greatest putter.

John Andrisani
Gulfport, Florida

PREFACE

Have you ever wondered why there are so many different types of putting strokes? How many different strokes have you attempted? How many different types of putters have you used to try and make those strokes work? If you watch the great players on television, you will see a wide variety of putting styles and putters. More often than not, the reason those great players have risen to the level of golf that they play is because of their unique putting strokes.

I have been playing and teaching golf for more than twenty years and have seen my share of unique putting strokes. Some work. Some never will. Because the majority of my students are not touring professionals, I have had to be creative in my instructional methods, and ironically, it was this creativity that led me to discover the true secret to good putting.

When I have watched, worked with, or played alongside great putters, I realized that, for whatever type of putting stroke they happened to be using, it worked great for them and they made it look simple. When you discuss with a great putter the secret of his or her success, you learn that it is not one secret but several. Great putters use customized putters. They read greens better than we can read the newspaper. They have figured out, to the detail, exactly which type of putting stroke and which set of mechanics to use to put the ball into the hole. They know exactly how to practice intelligently. They have full confidence in their abilities, and they use proven strategies for every circumstance.

Once I learned that great putters are not necessarily encyclopedias of putting knowledge, I was able to rethink how I was conveying my knowledge to my students. One secret to improving a player's putting prowess is to make sure that he or she is using a stroke and putter that best fits. The player must also understand the importance of creating consistency, learn a basic set of mechanics for his or her stroke, purposely apply the mental skills, and learn to read the greens. My approach to teaching putting does not make for a miracle overnight fix, but it does create better putters in a relatively short period.

Did you know that putting is the most important shot in golf? Why else would people say, "Drive for show and putt for dough"? I know putting is the most important shot, but I also believe the putt can be one of the easiest shots. A multitude of golfers do not see it that way because they have learned so much putting information that they do not know how to put it together and use it to sink putts. I do not think it is the player's fault. I think it is the way the golf world teaches the game. Whether on purpose or by accident, players receive information and tips on putting almost everywhere they turn: on television, in magazines and books, on the Internet, and from players in their weekend foursome. The problem for average players is that they do not know what to believe or what is truly going to help them putt better.

This book is a compilation of what I would consider to be great lessons on putting. My teaching methods are learned from the traditional, but I have evolved them to fit not just tour players, but any player. My teaching techniques are creative, which allows for individual uniqueness. The traditional way of thinking only allows for an idealized version. This is not a book about a single method of putting. It is about eight types of putting strokes. The book examines the details and offers how-tos of each putting stroke to help you find one that will work for you.

I believe anyone can learn to be a great putter. Just like the best putters, you should learn the importance of a custom-fit putter. You should understand that consistency is created. You need to learn a basic set of mechanics and the mental skills that allow the mechanics to perform. You need to learn the advantages of properly reading a green. And you should learn what and how to practice.

Because I am not there to give you personal one-on-one putting lessons, I will explain each important element of putting and then give you necessary guidelines. There is no substitute for a great teacher, but if you learn the information within, you'll have everything you need to become your own.

ACKNOWLEDGMENTS

I need to thank first the thousands of players I have observed putting. If not for some great putting I have witnessed with the many different strokes used, I think I would still be trying to teach the same old putting stroke to everyone. It was the players who really showed me that there is not just one ideal stroke to make putts. There are many ideal strokes, and each individual needs to find his or her personal ideal.

I would like to especially thank John Andrisani for helping to make this project a reality. Your insight and vast knowledge, as well as your editing skills, gave me the edge I needed for completing this valuable book on the strokes of putting. Thank you, Bobby Grace, for spending a rainy Florida morning answering my questions. I really appreciate your passing on some of your knowledge of the game of putting and its equipment. If only every dedicated player could have a conversation with you, they would realize just how important it is to have the right putter if they expect to improve their putting game. I was blessed to have the photographic talents of Yasuhiro "J.J." Tanabe. Here is a dedicated professional who took time away from photographing tour players to come and capture my thoughts on film. Thank you, J.J.

I thank my wife, Kami, and my daughters, Olivia and Averi, for sacrificing family time to allow for the great amount of work the book required. Thank you to my father, Brian Sr., for a last-minute photo shoot to complete the photo ensemble. Finally, Pasadena Y&CC deserves accolades for providing a beautiful golf course and venue for the photo shoot.

PUTT

LIKE A

PRO

WHAT IS THE MOST IMPORTANT SHOT IN GOLF?

Is hitting the golf ball 300 yards the most important shot in golf? Or a crisply struck long iron from 220 yards to within 15 feet of the hole? Or a beautifully swung short iron to 6 feet from the hole? Why not a pitch shot to get out of a bad position? Or a chip from the edge of the green? Could the most important shot be a soft-landing bunker shot? Or could it be the simple little putt? While each of these has its place and merit, to answer the question directly: *putting is the most important shot in golf.*

Putting is especially important if you are at all concerned with your final score. Consider the overall game of golf and its objective, which is to play your golf ball from a starting point to the bottom of a specific hole in as few shots as possible. Each individual shot, no matter the distance involved, the hazards faced, or the type of club used, has the same value on the scorecard: 1. Each and every shot has an equal value. The exceptions are penalty strokes. As there are penalties for each and every stroke at the ball, every shot still has the same potential value. So a shot is a shot is a shot.

I realize that some shots, like a 300-yard drive, are more fun than others. Some shots, like an approach shot over a deep bunker, may feel more important than others. But when the game is over, each shot is just worth 1 on the scorecard. Of all these shots, which is the one we usually end up using to finish the hole? The putt. On occasion, we may chip one in or hole one out from the fairway. On a great day we may even hole one from the tee for a hole-in-one. Unless luck is endlessly on our side, though, we are going to have to finish the hole with a putt.

Furthermore, to really appreciate the vital importance of putting, examine the following statistics of a typical eighteen-hole round. Wood play is 25 percent of the game; finesse wedges, 13 percent; short irons, 6 percent; medium irons, 5 percent; trouble shots, 5 percent; long irons, 3 percent; and putting, 43 percent. As you can see, for an eighteen-hole round of golf, most of the score can be directly attributed to putting, which is why I rank its importance above all others. Whether you simply want to make your days of golf more enjoyable or you are aspiring to beat the greatest players in the world, your best option is to improve your putting game. Take your own statistics and prove to yourself just how important putting is to your game. During your next round, track the total number of putts you made. Divide the number of putts by your total score. This will give you the percentage of shots that you used putting.

PUTTING DEFINED

If you want to master putting and lower your scores, it would make good sense if you begin to understand putting, its characteristics, and what defines putting perfection. If you understand putting, you will learn just how important, or unimportant, it is to be born a masterful putter. To begin, we need to clearly define its meaning. According to Webster's dictionary, the definition of *putting* is "a light stroke made on a green to get the ball into the hole." This definition is much too simplistic and vague. I figured I could find a better definition from someone who actually plays golf, so I went to the local country club and asked some of the players to define *putting*. The best interpretation I heard was that "it is the part of the game where madness begins and the hole eventually ends." Unfortunately, as insightful as that might be, it doesn't really suit our needs. I suspected someone who actually makes a living at playing golf might have a good definition, so I asked a tournament professional, who explained it as "a stroke on the putting green, made with a putter, to putt the ball into or close to the hole." That was a little better but still not as specific as I thought it could be. I did find a more precise definition from someone who not only makes his living from golf but also is a scientist turned famous golf instructor. Dave Pelz defines *putting* as "any stroke made with the putter, in which the player uses a normal putting stroke." I find this definition still lacking clarity. Based on my experience as a professional player, professional golf instructor, and student of the game and with all of my research on putting, I have assembled what I believe to be the most accurate definition to date: "the act of purposefully rolling a golf ball with a golf club over a specific distance along a selected path." Let us hope that at the end of the particular distance and path is the hole we have aimed for.

By definition, the biggest difference between putting and all of the other shots is purposefully rolling the golf ball. Because of this difference, some say putting is actually a game within the game of golf. The object of golf, once again, is to play your golf ball from a starting point to the bottom of a specific hole in as few shots as possible. The playing field of golf, the golf course, is one that challenges your ability to go that particular distance and direction. With a great number of obstacles along the way, the simple game of going from point A to the hole requires the player to move the ball in a number of different patterns, or golf shots. The drive for distance shots; irons for approach shots; pitches for delicate lofted shots; chips for low running shots; punch shots for lower ball flight; lobs for very high and quickly stopping shots; draws, fades, hooks, slices, high or low shots off the fairway grass; shots from the rough, woods, bunkers, pine needles, or hills; and, finally, shots on the putting green—while all of these shots aim to accomplish the same basic objective, putting is the one shot that most likely puts the ball to the bottom of the hole.

So is putting a game within a game? My answer is yes. To master the game of golf, you must master putting. Putting is how you accomplish your goal, while all of the other shots simply put you into a position to do so. Golf, to me, is a series of different games all bundled into one extremely interesting and complex package. My personal satisfaction from playing golf is the joy of winning one or more of those games during a round of eighteen holes. I play the drive as a game and approach shots, short-game shots, and putting each as a game, with the occasional "get-out-of-trouble" game thrown in. Each of these games has its own strategies and techniques to master, which is what keeps bringing me back. To master the putting game, you will need to learn all of the strategies, skills, and techniques unique to putting and unique to yourself.

All golf shots have their own characteristics. A bunker shot looks and plays nothing like a shot from off a tee, which looks and plays nothing like a six-foot putt. The differing characteristics are created by using different tools (clubs) and different methods of motion (golf swings) with which to make a stroke at the ball. Different clubs and different swings obviously will make the ball do different things. The most important feature of our putting definition is the fact that the ball rolls. Every club has the capability of making the ball roll. Have we not all had the experience of trying to hit that mighty long drive, maybe to impress the other players in a foursome? With the club descending toward the ball, some out-of-sync part of our body moves incorrectly, causing the club to strike the top of the ball, creating the not-so-beautiful "worm burner." Instead of driving the ball hundreds of yards, we roll it dozens of feet. This not-so-welcomed technique will cause a ball to roll, but it is definitely not the most consistent method to use on the putting green when you are trying to hole a putt. Distance-control issues come to mind.

We do know that the look of a putt is one of rolling. But is a putt a putt if it is not done from on the putting green? How far from the hole can you be and still have a putt? If you use your putter, is it automatically a putt? If you use a club other than your putter, can it be called a putt? All very important questions to answer if we are to have a complete understanding of putting.

Is a putt a putt if it is not done from on the putting green? The answer to this is yes. The reason is that a putt is a shot that is *intended* to roll. Just because your ball is not lying on the green does not mean that you cannot purposefully roll your golf ball. The term we golfers use for this type of putt is *Texas wedge*. There are circumstances when rolling your ball is not the best option, but then there are times when it is. For instance, say your ball has ended up on a nicely mown fringe, three feet from the edge of the putting surface. The fringe is smooth, and although it has taller grass than the green, it will accept a rolling ball nicely. So a good shot choice would be a putt. Some fringes can be inches in width, whereas others may be yards wide. You can certainly choose to putt on them. It all depends on the course that you are playing. Another situation could be that you hit a good approach shot and your ball has ended up only 12 feet from the hole. Unfortunately, it is in the rough just off the green. Even though you are close to the hole and could choose to use your putter, it would be impossible to roll the ball out of the high grass without having it jump and bounce. A jump and bounce is not a roll and, therefore, not a putt. (See Figure 1.1.)

How far from the hole can you be and still have a putt? It all depends on the size of the putting green and the condition and grass height of the fringe. There are putting greens that measure 200 yards from one end to the other. The thirteenth hole at Montgomerie Golf

1.1. A bouncing ball is considered a chip, even if a putter is used. The shot here, from the rough with a putter, is not considered a putt.

Club in Dubai comes to mind. Add a manicured fringe with low grass height and you could have a putt of incredible distance. There is a distance where the amount of power needed to strike the putt will cause the ball to fly and bounce. The height of the flight might be a mere couple of inches, but it is enough to reclassify the shot as a chip. As long as the ball rolls within the first few feet of a 20-foot or longer stroke without excessive bouncing, then I would consider it a putt. The maximum distance will vary from player to player, because proper technique is required from long distances to have the ball roll properly. Improper technique will cause the ball to bounce and/or fly, creating an unwanted chip instead of a putt.

If you use your putter, is your shot automatically a putt? No. Although the putter is beautifully designed to make the ball roll, certain swing techniques can make the ball move differently than a roll. One technique is to use the putter in a manner that hits the ball downward into the ground at an angle. When the ball is struck into the ground, it will rebound off of the ground and then bounce a few times before it slows and finally rolls. This shot is typically used from bad lies around the putting green where a lofted shot would be difficult if not impossible. (See Figures 1.2 and 1.3.) Another technique, which is not considered a putt and depends upon the style of putter used, is one where the ball comes to rest inches from a tree trunk and does not allow for a normal shot. For a right-handed player, the only option available to advance the ball toward the hole would be a left-handed shot. Some putters are designed with a flange at their back, which would allow for a left-handed strike at the ball.

1.2. You can use a putter creatively to hit a plugged ball out of the lip of a bunker.

1.3. Use the toe of your putter to blast it out in one attempt.

If you use a club other than your putter, can your shot be called a putt? Yes. There are rare circumstances when your putter may become unfit for play during a round (perhaps it was accidentally broken), yet you still need to somehow get the ball into the remaining holes. You will have to putt with one of your other clubs. You will have to modify your normal putting technique to allow the other chosen club to roll your ball. You can use any of the other clubs in place of your putter. One of the most common techniques is using a sand wedge. The sand

1.4. This is considered a putt, even though a sand wedge is being used. By hitting near the equator of the ball, you can create a putt with a wedge.

wedge is most often used because of its shorter length. By striking just above the equator of the ball with the lower edge (blade) of the sand wedge, you will cause the ball to roll, pretty much like a putt. (See Figure 1.4.) A second technique is to use a wood, which generally has the lowest amount of loft. Hold the club low on the grip (choke up), press the hands forward to reduce the loft further, and give it a putt.

If you tee off with your putter, is it a putt? There is only one instance that I can think of where this could be true. A putt could be a drive if you are playing miniature (putt-putt) golf!

To summarize, the game of putting, with its rolling-shot nature, can be played anywhere on the golf course and can be made with almost any of the clubs. It does have a distance restriction, but that will vary between players. Most of the time though, you are going to roll your putt from on the putting green with your putter, and this is what is truly important to master. You can be a putting master even if you do not perfect putting from a bunker.

PERFECT PUTTING

In most physical endeavors, to master the endeavor means to perform to perfection. Perfection in putting would mean holing every attempted putt in one try. Every time we played eighteen holes, we would have eighteen putts. This would be perfect putting. What is the chance of this happening? To calculate the odds would be an enormous undertaking, and most scientists are hopefully way too busy saving the world to work on a golf equation. I would love to be able to tell you that true putting perfection for all eighteen holes is possible each time you play, but it simply is not. Putting is a physical endeavor where mastery is achieved yet not at true perfection. Why? For one, we are merely human and make human errors, and two, we play the game out in nature with all of nature's unpredictability and inconsistencies. Not even golf's originators expected a level of putting perfection as true as one putt per hole.

Do you know what par stands for? *Par*, according to the *American Heritage Dictionary*, is "the number of golf strokes considered necessary to complete a hole or course." Usually par on any given hole is 3, 4, or 5. How was par decided upon? When the originators of golf set up golf courses, they created a par for each hole, based on true yardage and actually playing the newly made holes. When they established these pars, did they take putting into account? I believe they must have. Let us consider a par 3. Most par-3 holes are short in length and are easily within range for a possible hole out in one, so why allow for three shots? The reason is because putting is not easy. They figure that a par, the acceptable score for the hole, is achievable by hitting the first shot onto the putting surface and then allowing for two putts. One long shot and two putts equal a par 3 on this hole. The same scenario applies to a par-4 hole, except that two shots are allowed for in reaching the putting surface and again two putts to score a par. A par 5 is three shots to the green and another two putts. So based on the idea of making pars, which allow for two putts on every hole, can we have mastered putting if we hit all of the shots onto the greens in the proper number (regulation) and then hit two putts on every green?

If true putting perfection is one putt per hole, and we know that the originators allowed for two putts per hole, then actual mastery of putting must fall somewhere between the two. But this then gives us a fraction of putts per hole. Obviously, we cannot putt in fractions, so determining putting mastery must come from the statistics gained from putts made over a large number of holes. The two ways to gain the statistics needed to find putting mastery are from reviewing the performances of the best players in the world and from reviewing those results obtained by a scientific study.

A simile used for persons who seem to be performing a task to perfection, usually heard in the sports world for athletes playing at their best, is that he or she is performing like a machine. Would you agree that the true level of putting mastery could be discovered if a putting machine was invented that could have an absolutely consistent, repeatable, and dependable stroke, one that eliminates any human imperfection of body or mind and that can be taken onto the golf course and used to hit as many shots as possible to give reliable statistics? Fortunately for this discussion, that machine has already been invented. This machine, the True Roller (invented by Dave Pelz), rolls a golf ball a desired distance and in an exact direction every time, without the human error factor. What Pelz did was to take the device to different golf courses of varying upkeep and set it up it to make 12-foot putts. After 1,800 attempts at each course, his results (the percentage of shots successfully made) were as follows:

- ► Moderate-fee private country club with average conditions: 48 percent
- ► Moderate-fee private country club with good conditions: 54 percent
- ► Private country club with some of the country's best prepared putting greens: 84 percent

The moral of the story is what you'd expect: the less perfect the putting greens and nature, the more difficult it was to hole out putts, even for the perfect putting machine. This research illustrates that even if we are putting with the perfect putting tool and using a perfect golf ball, we possess the skills of an extraterrestrial, and we play on the most perfect greens our imagination can conceive of, we are still not going to be able to make every single putt in one shot. The machine does show us the importance of a putting green's condition to the chances you have of holing out putts from different distances. It also shows where putting mastery could be if we were as consistent and reliable as a machine.

As we are not machines, the real true measure to achieving putting mastery is in the capabilities of our fellow humans. The nature of golfers is to admire and study those players who have demonstrated that they are better than the rest, in hopes of discovering their secrets to success. Because golf has been played for hundreds of years, there are many great players who have been studied intensely and who will shed light on what human putting mastery is really about. Modern times puts the best putters performing their brilliance right in our living rooms, on our television sets. They are the players of the PGA, LPGA, Champions, and Nationwide tours. The PGA Tour features a collection of the greatest players in the world competing for some of the largest prize purses ever awarded.

The PGA Tour keeps statistics of all the putts and reveals humans' potential at putting mastery. Compare the following statistics with those of the True Roller, and see what a pro's potential is for putting. The best PGA pros have an average of around 1.7 putts per green hit in regulation and just under 28 total putts, or 1.55 putts per hole for all eighteen holes. It would be great to continue to demonstrate human putting mastery with individual statistics from specific distances, but those statistics have not been kept over the careers of the great putters to give us a truly accurate measure. Among the legendary players who had great reputations as masters of putting are Bobby Jones, Bobby Locke, Walter Hagen, Sam Snead, George Low, Walter Travis, George Archer, Arnold Palmer, Jack Nicklaus, Ben Crenshaw, and Tom Watson. Without solid statistics, it is hard to show just how well they had mastered putting. Based on their reputations, we can be sure that their statistics would have equaled their reputations.

Becoming a putting machine and holing every putt that you attempt would be as good as it gets. Unfortunately, you will not be able to eliminate the human element, which includes the need to consistently coordinate mind and body to perform precise and repeatable motions from shot to shot over eighteen holes, along with the application of so many different putting stroke techniques, tips, and advice on how to use those techniques, in addition to the emotions and egos that come with being human. We cannot control the natural elements of the game. Golf is played out in nature, an ever-changing and somewhat unpredictable environment that provides a surface that is neither level nor flat and results in conditions that are nearly impossible to control from day to day. The best we can strive for is to equal or better the best human putters.

Are PGA Tour players the only players to master putting? No. Anyone can master putting. If you have been around golf for any length of time, you have heard the stories or seen the local players who seem to make every putt they attempt. A masterful putter in my assessment is one who makes more putts on average than most other players. It comes down to pure statistics. If you have the right statistics, you earn the title of Master Putter. The best way to find your level of putting mastery is by tracking your putting statistics and comparing them to those of the best tour players.

WHERE GREAT PUTTERS COME FROM

There seems to be a question as to whether great putters are born or created. Some players, usually poor putters, feel that the only way to become a great putter is to be born into it. They have bought many putters, had a lesson or two, and read a hundred different tips on putting, yet they never improve. This lack of success in contrast to the amount of effort they feel they have put in reinforces their notion that if you are a great putter, it had to be god-given talent. Poor putters will usually just give in to the thought and use the born-into-it theory as an excuse for their poor efforts.

It is my belief that great putters are created. Players with the proper desire, appropriate instruction, and dedication to the traits that make a great putter can achieve their goals regardless of birthright. If you study the great players, you will find, like I did, that they all possess certain traits that make them great putters. If you dedicate yourself to learning and using these traits, you, too, will evolve into a great putter. These common traits are:

- ► Mastering the fundamentals and skills of putting
- ► Possessing great knowledge of reading greens
- ► Using a putting stroke of one type or another that properly fits your unique features
- ► Playing with a custom-fit putter
- ► Practicing perfectly within a routine
- ► Making more putts than the majority of golfers

If a good or great putter is who you want to become, then it is up to you to create the good habits required to acquire the traits. As a teaching professional, I have seen countless amateurs and touring professionals—great, good, and poor putters included—and what I have learned from them is that to be successful at putting, you must pick a stroke, stick to your routines, and develop the required skills. The most skillful putters, by following routines, have turned great putting into a habit—a multitude of habits actually, each designed to improve their chances. Psychologists claim that habits can be learned after just two weeks of consistent attention, and while I am not implying that you can master putting in only two weeks, I do believe that we all have the potential to reach our ground-game goals in a relatively short period of time and become great putters—regardless of the level of natural talent we bring with us.

WHY DO MOST PLAYERS FAIL TO IMPROVE THEIR PUTTING GAME?

Even after buying an assortment of the hottest putters on the market; taking a formal lesson or two from a PGA professional; or practicing putting for countless hours in the office, at home on the rug, or on your country club's practice green, why does significant improvement still always seem out of reach? Wouldn't it be more fun if you could make more putts when you really needed to? Most players don't improve because of the following:

► Instructors are stuck with antiquated teaching methods and do not think outside the box enough to come up with solutions for each individual's needs.
► The golf media overemphasizes the mechanics of putting and does not address strongly enough the remaining elements of good putting, like green reading.
► Golf manufacturers focus on target markets, not necessarily each individual.
► Players try in vain to find the answers through all of the confusion.

INSTRUCTORS DO NOT EVOLVE

First, there are those instructors simply in the position of giving lessons to supplement their meager paychecks. This mentality obviously works against the player's best interests, making it especially difficult for him or her to make serious improvements to his or her putting game. This type of instructor will likely teach standard basics and styles of putting regardless of a student's uniqueness. Sometimes these instructors will attempt to teach the technique that they actually use. They will also be looking to find the quickest fix, or bandage, that will give the player immediate short-term results. The player leaves the lesson satisfied from those positive short-term results but over a longer period will find that he or she has not actually made a permanent correction or improvement.

Next, there are the instructors who may have an earnest intent to help the player but do not have the golf education or teaching knowledge to provide the best long-term results. These instructors will teach ideas that have worked for their games or that they learned in their short careers. They try their best to pass on tips to students. This effort may help the players. The problem is that the typical teacher lacks the resources or knowledge to properly educate players in the true needs of permanent putting improvement for each player's unique differences.

And finally, there are many good instructors trying honestly to help players improve their games. These instructors, having become accomplished players themselves, completely understand the mechanics of good putting and have learned to teach expertly. They may have even learned the art of instruction from other proven, quality teachers of the game. The big problem is that golf is a game of tradition, and a lot of these good instructors are going to continue to teach the same material that has been instructed for a hundred years. A lot of the information they teach is great. It just does not fit all of the players all of the time.

There are so many different types of players, with different body attributes and strokes, as well as different methods to use for putting a ball, that the age-old traditional method is not the only possibility.

What is needed is for more teachers to think creatively and help average players learn the proper style of putting for their individual needs and differences. Everyone has a perfect style for his or her putting needs. A good teacher needs to help a player find what works best specifically for him or her. Teachers also need to teach the entire putting game, from practicing the skills to having properly fitted equipment and golf balls, from reading greens properly to understanding and utilizing the mental game. I know from personal experience that not all players go to an instructor because they want to reinvent their putting games. Many want a quick miracle. It is the teacher's job not only to give the customer what he or she wants, which may be a quick fix for the day, but to also educate the player on the importance of being dedicated to permanent putting game improvement. A great teacher will pass on a deeper understanding of what is truly involved in being a good putter. A great teacher will have to prove to and convince the player that permanent improvement is not a quick miracle but a series of properly learned and practiced adjustments. A lot of teachers find it easier to just give players the short-term fix, which is not what they really need.

THE GOLF MEDIA FOCUSES ON MECHANICS

The golf media's ultimate success comes from providing its product to as many subscribers and viewers as possible in order to attract valuable advertisers and to sell profit-making advertising space and airtime, month after month. Even though they may have their hearts in the right place, which is to help golfers better their game, many media outlets are multimillion-dollar businesses that must meet a bottom line and provide products that create repeat customers. There are basically three different types of media that affect the putting game: television, print media, and the Internet.

TV is all about filling airtime. Airtime is valuable, as there are millions of viewers watching at the same time. Therefore, the TV media must provide programming that will appeal to the majority and keep the number of viewers high. This means that any type of putting instruction offered must fit into a predetermined time slot between commercials and must be appealing enough not to lose viewers. Any instructor doing his or her craft on TV can attest that the way to speak to the masses and maintain their attention is to keep the information basic and try to say it in a way that is new and intriguing. Golf swing mechanics can be broken down into many specific movements. A particular mechanical movement can also be taught in many different ways, which can give the instructor the ability to teach the same specific movement over and over again but seem to the viewer to be teaching something different. Teaching on TV is very much like teaching a clinic at the country club. You will have a large variety of skill levels and playing types among your students. As we teachers know, you can never go wrong focusing on the basic mechanics. If you can teach the basic mechanics in a way the player has never heard, you have passed on new information and will be perceived as a great teacher. Also, just like in a clinic, teachers will find it difficult to give individual attention to a specific student, and when a teacher attempts to instruct a student's particular need in front of the crowd, the other students will either attempt to utilize this knowledge for their own game, even if it has nothing to do with their improvement, or they will just lose focus. This usually leads to confusion and possibly a misunderstanding of what the instructor was trying to convey.

A second area of the TV media that is causing putting improvement problems for players is the abundance of infomercials and commercials for putters, techniques, and training aids. These commercials are designed specifically to sell products. They offer great scientific reasons, personal testimonies, and other motivational techniques to get viewers at home to make the purchase. They will never tell you the reasons why you shouldn't use the product. All products are designed to help a particular player with a particular fault in his or her putting game. You may not be the person it was designed to help. But then again, you might be. This all adds to the confusion about exactly how best to permanently improve your putting. Remember that the TV media has limited time and a broad audience and thus cannot go into the specific details needed for putting improvement for each individual. The point is to simply make sure the audience is entertained, not necessarily instructed.

Print media, mainly magazines, due to the need to attract readers, is similar to the TV media in many regards. It also has a large and varied audience and will need to provide enough advice and information to attract the reader to the next installment. The best way to attract repeat customers is to give them what they want, but only enough so that they need to come back for more next time. Players want tips to improve their game, and mechanics can always cause some type of small, mostly short-term improvement. Again, coming up with new ways to discuss mechanics is an easy topic, one that most readers enjoy. If all the player gets is incomplete information all of the time, he or she cannot see the big, complete picture. It would be like purchasing a ten thousand–piece puzzle, but you only get one piece a month for the rest of your life, and you do not even know what the final picture really looks like. Furthermore, the company may be sending you some wrong pieces. To top it all off, your friends keep giving you some of their extra pieces. There is a lot of good information that can be gleaned from reading. The problem is, it is hard for the media to fit in all of the information that is needed and to provide the individual attention that is needed for serious improvement within a format designed for quick reading and entertainment.

The Internet is a venue that contains endless information. If you have a question, there probably is a website waiting for you to log on and provide you with an answer. The Internet is not necessarily stuck on mechanics geared for a wide audience, even though some individual websites might be. It is a media outlet where people can find just about any information they need. You may actually have a better chance at finding individual advice geared for you on the Internet than anywhere else. But how do you determine if it is designed for your putting or for someone else's? How can you verify that your source is credible? Someday the Internet may just become the best place to learn golf, as it has the potential to house custom content and let viewers search by their needs—but there's still a long road left to travel before that happens.

MANUFACTURERS DO NOT FOCUS ON INDIVIDUALS

Manufacturers, when it comes to putters, have an endless opportunity to be creative. Various different materials can be used for putter heads. These include most metals, as well as glass, stone, synthetics, or plastics, each of which produces a different effect. You can find makers of putters on a small scale that do a really great job at customizing putters for individuals, but unfortunately the large manufacturers contribute to many putting woes. The big-brand equipment makers have profit margins to maintain, which means they need hot products to sell and they need manufacturing methods that keep their costs low. The best way for putter sales to skyrocket is for the manufacturer to come up with a catchy design, a great tour golfer to win a tournament with the putter, and an assembly line to then produce exact copies all day long. Manufacturers ship all of these copies to golf shops worldwide, which makes sure that players can get their hands on the hottest putters quickly right off the shelf. There may be nothing wrong with these products, but unless your individual needs happen to match up with the design and fitting variables, chances are there's nothing right with them either. Players have learned to simply keep buying putters until one magically works one day. How many putters do you own?

PLAYERS TRY TO FIND ANSWERS IN CONFUSION

If players continue to count on teachers stuck in the box and not committed to long-term improvement, rely on the media to offer the miracle tip that will cure their woes, and trust the large manufacturers with their marketing campaigns as to what putters to purchase, they will never become great putters.

Armed with the truth, how do we make long-term improvements to our putting games? For players to dramatically advance their putting games, I suggest they start with an understanding of the following. (Those elements that have not already been discussed will be explored in the chapters to come.)

- ► Players need to have their own putting style that fits their individual personalities and physical attributes.
- ► Players need to be convinced—not by manufacturers but by fellow players and respected instructors—that putting equipment must be properly fit for each player and each player's unique putting style and unique physical attributes.
- ► Players need to understand that nature and the ball affect a rolling golf ball on its way toward the hole. Nature is the natural effects of the putting green, such as grass height and condition, hills, bumps, and valleys. Seeing and understanding these effects are what golf-

PUTT LIKE A PRO

ers call reading greens. The ball itself has possible condition issues, such as roundness and balance.

► Players need to realize that the skills of putting are not just the physical mechanics of striking a putt. The skills also include the mental game skills of concentration, strategy, and confidence.

► Players need to effectively practice their putting game. They should spend an equal amount of time between putting and the full-swing shots. During an effective practice session, proper drills, appropriate mechanical fixes, green reading, strategy, and confidence building need to be addressed and focused on.

I don't think there is a player anywhere who doesn't want to improve his or her game. Now that you have learned the truth, you can begin to effectively find the answers to guaranteed putting improvement.

THE BASICS: MENTAL SKILLS
AND CONSISTENCY

Despite the individuality of putting, great putters must conform to
a set of basic skills in order to successfully putt from day to day and
throughout their career. Most people believe those skills are tied to
some form of mechanic, such as keeping the head down. Even though
keeping your head down may be a seemingly important mechanical
factor for some strokes, it is not one of the basic skills. I believe that
too many players fail to greatly improve their putting because most of
their focus is on the physical mechanics. Even more so, the mechanical
actions can be very different between the individual strokes used for
putting. Some players will work on improving mechanics of one stroke,
while unknowingly practicing and playing with a different stroke alto-
gether, on which the mechanics they have been working on have no
bearing. The basic skills apply to all strokes, regardless of individual
stylings. I call the four basic putting skills the mental skills, the skill
of creating consistency, the physical skills (which include the putting
laws and the basic mechanics of controlling the putt's starting direction and controlling distance), and the skill of reading greens.

I always like to introduce the importance of the mental skills and the need to practice and play with them first while working toward mastery of the putting stroke. Most amateurs, because of their lack of understanding of the mental game, blame poor putting on some form of mechanical malfunction. In fact, good mechanics can be ruined by poor mental skills. This is because inadequate mental skills can truly limit a player's ability to execute his or her physical skills and perform to his or her potential. It does not matter how good your physical skills are—if your mental skills are poor, your putting will absolutely be poor.

I like to make sure that players completely understand the skill of creating consistency. Without consistency, a player's learning process and improvement forecast will be a long adventure with quite a few stormy times. With consistency, a player is best prepared to retain and build on the progress he or she makes.

Next are the physical skills. (See Chapter 4.) I feel this is the step where most players get stuck because they do not learn the proper fundamentals of putting, they do not understand that there are differences in mechanics among the different types of putting strokes, they do not learn that the mechanics are only important to the point of accomplishing specific distance and directional skills, and they do not know when to stop focusing on mechanics and when to move their attention to the other skills. You can't completely master your physical skills until you learn the mental skills.

Finally, the skill of reading greens comes into play. (See Chapter 5.) Without being able to read a green, you will never be able to hole putts consistently no matter how well you have mastered the other skills.

When attacking the task of improving your putting skills, you have to decide which of the skills to work on first. Before you make that decision, I recommend that you read through the rest of this chapter as well as Chapters 4 and 5 to make sure that you have a solid understanding of each skill. Even though I believe that the four skills are all equally important, I have found that the best players will master the mental skills first, while they are still improving their physical skills. They then address consistency so they can completely master the physical skills. The final skill they master will be reading greens. This is because to really master reading greens, you need to learn all of the variables that affect a rolling ball, which requires the experience gained by playing different courses, under different conditions, in varying regions throughout the world.

Once you have read through the three chapters that cover the four skills, you can then decide which skill to work on first. This may vary based on your experience level coming in; beginners will simply follow the pattern of the best putters, whereas others might recognize the areas in which they need the most improvement and start there. For the sake of simplicity, I have presented the skills in the same order in which I first listed them, but feel free to jump around as you see fit. No matter what level player you are, you must dedicate yourself to improvement by working hard on your skills, not just by spending your time looking for a miracle tip.

THE MENTAL SKILLS

If you do not consider mastering the mental skills a priority, you may as well give up your attempt to master putting. Mastering the mental skills requires no technical abilities or mechanics and doesn't even require physically touching the ball. But this skill is just as important as the other basic skills. Some experts claim that the game of golf is 85 percent mental. With this being said, I feel the mental skills actually dictate how good a putter you are. If you have poor mental skills, no matter how good your physical skills may be, you will on the whole be a poor putter. Your physical skills may prop you up for a single putt, but over the long haul, you'll need strong mental abilities to regularly sink key shots.

Have you ever considered practicing the mental game? Do you know what the mental skills are as they apply to putting? Traditionally, golf instruction has mainly focused on mechanics, leaving the mental skills to hopefully develop on their own. I feel this tradition exists because the definition and the basic components of the mental game are not clearly understood. I define the mental game as being the use and control of one's thoughts to effectively allow the muscles to execute an effective golf shot.

I consider the mental skills to be a combination of strategy, concentration, and confidence. Some of the basic errors caused by mental skill deficiencies in putting are missing putts of less than three feet and taking three or more putts from closer than 20 feet from the hole. In order for the mental game to be successful, all three elements must work together. If your confidence and strategy are excellent but you are concentrating on something other than the hole, then your putting game will suffer. Likewise, if your strategy and concentration are good but you lack confidence, you will most likely make mistakes. The method to mastering your mental game is to build up the three mental skills components, apply the practices of each skill to your putting game, and continuously evaluate and practice your mental skills to arrive at the level where you have full control of them under all circumstances.

Strategy

Strategy is a mental skill that everyone is capable of mastering. It is the skill you start to use before you even strike your first putt of the day. There are many putting strategies to employ and things to consider in deciding which shall be a factor in your game. To be consistent you will want to know what strategy will be best for you on any given day. Following is a list of different types of issues in need of a strategic solution.

► **Fast or slow greens.** When you play on greens that are faster or slower than you are accustomed to, a good strategy is to spend a little extra time on the practice green before you start, simply focusing on your distance control. During play, if you still do not have a great feel for the distance, depending on whether you are leaving the putts short or long, start aiming at spots other than the hole. For instance, if you are leaving putts a foot too short, look for a spot a foot and a half beyond the hole, and try to get your ball to stop there.

► **Skills issues and mechanical problems.** Practicing to eliminate skills issues is the best strategy, but sometimes these arise just before you start playing. You will have to adjust the strategy for dealing with skills issues during play depending on the specific type of issue. The best strategy is normally to play with whatever the problem may be and just allow for it. If the problem is a pull, for example, aim a bit farther out than you would normally to allow for it. In other words, as opposed to fighting the problem while you're playing or trying to make big changes on the fly, work with it.

► **Terrain issues.** If you happen to be playing a course with a different terrain than you are used to, you need to be able to make adjustments. Most of the time, different terrain will cause problems reading the green. The best strategy is to seek out local knowledge of how best to read the local terrain. For example, playing on a golf course in mountainous terrain will cause reading issues due to the elevation changes. Greens in this terrain are hard to visually read. The local knowledge would be that all the greens would generally break away from the mountain peak and toward the valley. So your strategy would be to always look for the mountain peak and the valley and to then try to see how the ball will roll given that knowledge.

► **Confidence levels.** Sometimes you may lack confidence in your putting. You will definitely need a strategy if this is the case. The strategy you should take will depend on whether you are lacking confidence in your distance control, your accuracy, or both. For lack of confidence in distance control, the best strategy is simply to practice. If for whatever reason that's not an option or practice does nothing to restore your confidence, then your best strategy will be to widen your distance target. By this I mean, for long putts, instead of trying to precisely land your ball at the hole or 18 inches beyond, make your area of success a four-foot circle around the hole. Consider a success any ball that lands within the circle. After having a number of successes, reduce the width of the circle by a foot. Hopefully, by the end of the round, you will have had enough success to give you hope.

If your accuracy is the issue, then again your best strategy is practice. If you are playing and your confidence in regard to accuracy falls, then choose a spot two or three feet in front of the ball and aim for it. Align your putter and make sure your grip is correct and your body and feet are aligned. Once everything is aligned, focus only on your distance control. Stroke the putt, and before you look up, tell yourself by feel whether the putt was long, short, or just right. Once you feel what distance you made, then look up. By focusing only on your distance control, you will have less time to worry about the direction. If you have aligned everything correctly to begin with, then you really should be focusing only on distance anyway. Once the round is over, go practice your accuracy until you regain your confidence.

Any of many different strategies can be quite effective for your putting game. The point for the moment is not to teach you these specific strategies (although you're welcome to use them); rather, the point is to instill within you the idea that having a strategy to deal with the many variables that could affect your putting is a requirement of a strong, mentally skilled player. Without a strategy, you are simply not going to improve. So whenever you are confronted with an issue, take an extra moment to devise a strategy to overcome the issue, and stick with the strategy throughout. If you're wrong, learn from it. The process will definitely improve your mental skills and lower your scores. In the following I have outlined a few strategies you can use for dealing with some basic issues.

▶ **Strategies for different types of games.** You can use different strategies for putting for different games you might play. For normal stroke play games, strategies will vary depending on how many holes are left to play and where you may stand scorewise. You may want to putt more conservatively early in the round and later play more aggressively, with even more risk taking as the game comes to an end. If you are leading by many shots, then you may stay conservative the whole way. In match play, your putting strategy can change from hole to hole, depending on how the hole is being played out. Obviously, if you need to two-putt to win the hole, your strategy is pure distance control. If you need to one-putt to tie, total aggressiveness is the strategy. If you play in scramble tournaments, a team strategy is needed. Your first putter should be your most conservative putter. This player will show the line of the putt more consistently than an aggressive putter will. You want your aggressive putters to putt second and third, with your cleanup putter the best overall putter of the team. The fourth putter, if still needed to putt, will be able to determine whether to play conservatively or aggressively based on the results of the prior players.

▶ **Strategies for different weather conditions.** Different weather conditions call for differing strategies. Great weather requires no extra strategy, unless you usually play in the rain. Rainy, windy, and snowy weather all need to be played differently. Playing in the rain will require hand- and putter-drying routines before you stroke your putt and the ability to identify puddles in the intended line with the appropriate green-reading alterations to accommodate puddle depth. Wind may require an alteration to mechanics to steady oneself. By widening your stance, you will lower your center of gravity and give yourself a more secure base with better balance. Another strategy is to wait for a momentary lull in the wind before striking the putt. This strategy can disrupt your rhythm, though.

► **Strategies for playing with undesirable partners.** Sometimes you may get paired with someone that you do not enjoy playing with for some reason or another. This requires a strategy, or else you will be bothered completely out of your game. If you are riding carts, make sure that you are in a different cart to keep your interactions at a minimum. When I have been in this position, while approaching the putting green, I would grab my putter and approach the green on my own, either ahead of the troublesome player or lagging behind. I would then concentrate on my putt and go about my business with as little interaction as possible. It is not proper to be rude or disrespect-ful, but it is not improper to focus on your game. As I said, as little interaction as possible. Some interaction will probably happen. If it happens on the green, you will need to collect your thoughts before putting. Some players, prior to addressing the ball, will crouch behind their ball, staring at the hole. More than likely they are trying to erase a bad past episode and regain their focus.

► **Strategies for dealing with pace-of-play problems.** Sometimes you will be paired in or behind a group that is playing at a slower pace than your norm. If you do not have a strategy, this pace will likely throw your game into a tailspin. In slow-play situations, the best strategy is to avoid thoughts of the pace and how badly it messes up your game. Focus instead on when you need to concentrate on your putt and when you need to redirect your attention to something else. Pepole have different things they can do while wasting time between shots. Slow play means you have a little more time to waste than normal. If you think about it, even at your normal pace, there are times between shots that you will not be focusing on your next shot. What do you do during those downtimes? In a slower-pace situation, those in-between times are a little lengthier. That means you need to stretch out your in-between shot focus. I am somewhat artistic, so when it is not my shot or time to concentrate on the shot, I enjoy scanning the property to look for scenes that might be interesting to paint someday. Golf is played in the most beautiful settings, and when given the time, I like to enjoy my day and take time to smell the roses along the way. I also enjoy playing eighteen holes in two and a half hours, which gives me the rest of the day to enjoy in other ways. My game is consistent though, whether it lasts two and a half hours or six hours, because I employ an effective strategy.

► **Everyday strategy.** Most of the time, you will probably be playing golf at the same course under the same conditions, so you will not face too many differing situations that require different strategies—instead, you need an everyday strategy. This is one that you use over and over to create consistency and to help avoid complacency. A lot of players assume that conditions will be exactly the same each and every day, and this can cost them strokes. So be wary. You may have played the same course ten days in a row under the same conditions, but tomorrow the superintendent might need to maintain the greens with some preventive measure, altering them in the process. If you use an everyday strategy, such a change will not shock you and cause a bad round. You will be better prepared to handle the change, no matter how slight or significant. Having an everyday strategy simply means to follow your green-reading procedures without fail, plan to do the same pregame routine every day, and execute your motions with confidence, the same way every day.

To master the mental skill of strategic play, you will need to practice. Practicing the skill of strategic play, though, is not what you may think of as normal practice. Think about a football team and how the players practice. A football practice has several different components. There are field practices, gym practices, and meeting room practices. Some practices are for improving the body, others are for developing individual position skills, others are for improving fundamental mechanics, and still others are for practicing being a team. A big part of practice for football is defining strategy. Whether it is done in the film room studying past results or on the field practicing the plays believed to be most effective against the team's next opponent, the deliberate nature of each decision is all a part of strategy. If you have not been practicing your strategies, then you are missing out on an important part of your practice. Your strategies for dealing with situations are what prevent you from flying blind, and your first step in developing golf strategies to practice is to review your rounds. You can record statistics and notes during or after play, or even have someone videotape you as you make your way around the course. Whatever method you use, you need to think about the strategies that you have used and how successful (or unsuccessful) they were.

The hardest part about developing strong strategies is maintaining them. You need to decide on your strategies, make a game plan for your next round, and do your best to stick to it. Following your round, a good review will tell you how well your strategies worked. If you do not stick to your strategies for the entire round, you really will not have enough feedback to determine whether the strategies were at fault or if the problem was because of something else. I recommend that you write out your strategies before you play. After the round, review what you wrote and chart the results. This will give you a history of the strategies you have used and their successes and failures. Review these during your strategy practices to help you better prepare for future rounds.

Concentration

Concentrate is to focus completely on the task at hand. The dictionary definition of *concentration* is "give full attention." This skill is the ability to focus and give your full attention to the upcoming putt. For every putt, there are two different times when concentration is needed: reading the green and making the stroke. Some players think concentration is required all the way around the course. It is not. If you know when to turn your concentration on and off, you will have mastered this skill.

For each attempt, we have learned that we need to read the greens and then use our skills to make the stroke. Concentration is needed for both if you want to be successful. The time to concentrate is when you decide to start reading the green and all the way through the green-reading process until you have solved all of the variables and chosen the path you want your ball to travel. Once you have done this, you can relax until it is time for you to make your stroke. Once you decide to make your stroke, you need to concentrate again, from the start of your preshot routine until the stroke is completed and the ball is rolling away from you. The concentration skill is simply focusing on the job at hand, while avoiding outside distractions as well as the distractions of your own thoughts.

Outside Distractions. These are birds, animals, cars, trucks, planes, workers, other players, caddies, and any other distraction that exists outside of you. What the great putters do when they are confronted with an outside distraction is to stop what they are doing at the exact moment of the distraction (this might even be during the back or down stroke of the putt), acknowledge the distraction, and then assess its duration. If it stops right away, good players simply restart their routine from the beginning. If the distraction is not going to stop, players will use their mental skill of concentration to turn the distraction into background noise and then restart their routine. Have you ever seen players who seem to be distracted by all kinds of minor disturbances, like a bird singing its song? We say these types of players have rabbit ears. They are very easily distracted. They lack the mastery of the mental skill of concentration. Have you seen players who seem to be able to putt successfully even when a loud distraction occurs during their putt? These players are not oblivious; they just know how to concentrate on the task at hand. To concentrate properly when there are outside distractions you should do the following:

- ► Refocus your attention on the upcoming putt.
- ► Focus completely on the steps of your routine.
- ► Follow each step of your routine with little delay between the steps. Any extra delay will allow your mind to wander, which is when you will most likely get distracted.
- ► If you get distracted again, simply start over and refocus again.

A lot of times it is hard to concentrate. This is why concentration is a skill. The better you learn to concentrate under all circumstances, the better a putter you will become. Do not use distractions as an excuse for a poor putt. Use distractions as a gauge to how well you are mastering the mental skill of concentration.

Your Own Thoughts. These distractions are your mind talking to your consciousness about anything other than what you are trying to accomplish. For example, instead of finishing reading the green, you begin thinking about what you will have for dinner, how well or poorly the day is going, or if you are going to miss or make the putt. A second example concerns swing thoughts, which are the specific ideas that you are thinking to create the mechanical movements of the stroke. At their most beneficial, they represent one specific concept that you have chosen to emphasize. The distraction occurs either when too many swing thoughts have free rein in your head or when any one of those thoughts is incorrect. You should learn to limit your swing thoughts to one or two basic ideas during the stroke of a putt.

To master this skill, you will need to learn how to eliminate distractions and what to do when a distraction occurs. A lot of times you can simply wait for an outside distraction to go away. Mental distractions require you to identify the distraction first and then have counterthoughts that block it out and place your mind back on a focused track to accomplishing your goals. When I find my mind wandering, I stop what I am doing, tell myself politely to shut up, focus on the shot, and then redirect my thoughts to my target and how I am going to get my ball there. I do not attempt a stroke until my wandering mind has become focused. Sometimes it takes a while, but not so long that it delays other players. What the great putters do when they are confronted with mental distractions is to stop what they are doing, acknowledge the distraction, determine the cause of the distraction, solve the cause of the distraction by counteracting the thought, and then restart the routine with proper concentration.

How many times while watching a pro on tour have you seen the player step away from the ball and begin muttering something just as he or she was about to make a stroke? This is a situation where the player has recognized his or her own distraction. It could be caused by a number of reasons (for example, the normal routine was not followed, the setup was slightly off, the value of the putt created thoughts of grandeur, the player's thoughts were simply off to another place, or he or she was second-guessing the green reading). Whatever the cause of the distraction, the player was able to recognize that his or her concentration was off—and his or her mental skill of concentrating prevented a bad putt from occurring. By stepping away at that moment, the player was able to find the cause of the distraction, block out the distraction with appropriate thoughts, and then continue forward with a positive putt attempt.

Finding the appropriate counteracting thoughts to mental distractions comes with experience. In practicing this skill, you want to be in tune with what you're thinking. You need to learn to recognize when your mind is distracted from a positive routine. The counteracting thoughts will have to relieve your concerns or sharpen your attention by focusing not on what could go wrong but on what you have to do to make it go right. Only you can control your mind and its distractions. This is a very important skill to master.

Confidence

Confidence is earned. The proper definition of *confidence* is "full trust." To be confident, as part of your mental game, is to trust your equipment, your green-reading abilities, and your physical skills. When you have full trust, you can make strokes at the ball with a clear mind, thereby allowing the physical skills (which hopefully you have practiced to the point that they have become routine) to perform to the level you desire. Confidence goes hand in hand with concentration. With confidence, you will be less likely to have negative thoughts. To gain confidence in all aspects of your game means that you must set your expectations, know what you are trying to accomplish, and know how to reach and exceed those goals. If your expectations do not match your abilities, then putting errors will likely occur and your confidence will be reduced. You should have clear expectations for all aspects of putting and for each putt.

▶ **Equipment.** Because you choose your equipment prior to play, your expectations for the equipment should be very high. You should expect perfection. If you expect less, your equipment may cost you extra putts.

▶ **Green reading.** Your expectations in regard to your green-reading skills should match your green-reading knowledge level. If you do not know the first thing about green reading and still expect to identify every line properly, you will become frustrated very quickly, leading to tension and making your physical skills even less effective, which may ultimately disrupt your confidence. If your green-reading knowledge is complete and you still do not expect to see the line every time, you probably will not (a self-fulfilling prophecy). When you match your expectations to your ability, you have the best chance to hole putts.

► **Physical skills.** Just as in green reading, when it comes to physical skills, your expectations need to match your skill levels. If your skill levels are excellent, then you need to be expecting to hole every putt. If you have beginner skill levels, you should expect less, even as you strive for more.

Once you are clear on your expectations, create confidence by knowing that you will reach or exceed your expectations. Have confidence in your equipment. If you have been custom fit for the proper putter, it matches your personal stroke and physical skills, it is properly designed for the types of greens that you play on, and you have all of the other putting equipment in place, then you should have full confidence that your equipment will help you to be a successful putter. Be confident in your green reading. Know the variables and do your best to interpret them for each putt. Having confidence in your green reading is essential to being a successful putter. Even if you cannot solve all of the variables for a particular putt, you still must decide on a line. Once you decide on a line, whether you have chosen correctly or not, you must be confident in your decision. This confidence will allow you to make your best effort. Never strike a putt until you have confidently decided on the line you want your ball to start. If it takes a little extra time to create your confidence in the line, take it. Be confident with your physical skills. Practice and experience are what breeds confidence in your physical skills. The more you tip the scale in favor of holed putts versus missed putts, the higher your confidence will be. There is no shortcut in gaining confidence with your physical skills. Remember the saying that practice makes perfect. Just remember that putting itself is rarely perfect. Even when you are missing putts, you must still convince yourself that all is well with your physical mechanics if you want to remain confident.

I once heard a story where the great Jack Nicklaus had finished a round of golf and was interviewed by a reporter who asked him if the three-putt he made on whatever hole had shaken his confidence. Mr. Nicklaus replied, "I never three-putt," and he proceeded to walk away. Whether the story is true or not, it does illustrate an example of a great player creating confidence. Whether things are going perfectly or not, the great players continue to think that things are going perfectly so as to maintain a high confidence level. Players who have not mastered this skill would simply wonder if perhaps that three-putt was the start of bad things to come, which would lead to less-than-perfect confidence levels. Not so for Mr. Nicklaus. Remember, he never three-putts.

THE SKILL OF CREATING CONSISTENCY

Creating consistency is the skill that allows players to advance to a higher level in their putting game by giving them the ability to tie up everything they learn into a uniform and repeatable routine. With consistency, no matter the length or difficulty of a putt, you will approach it in the same manner each and every time. To become consistent at putting you must be able to seamlessly combine your skills, both in practice and on the course. Of all the thousands of students I have worked with, the most common request for help that I get is, "How can you help me to become more consistent?"

All of the great putters are consistent, and what is unknown to most is that each and every one of them creates consistency as they develop, practice, and play. Consistency just does not appear one sunny day. I believe most players feel that if they can come up with a miracle tip, they will all of a sudden be consistent. It just does not happen like that. Consistency takes a purposeful and knowledgeable effort. If you do not stick to using the same routine from hole to hole and from round to round, you will never be consistent. An example of using an inconsistent routine is a situation we golfers have all faced: a meaningless three-foot putt for quintuple bogey. How much thought and effort did you put into making that putt? Now compare that to a three-foot putt for birdie and to win the hole. I guarantee you took your time, thought about the breaks and speed, and put all of your effort into assuring that the birdie putt was made. Did you make it? If you used the same routine for each, you would have used the same thoughts and amount of effort for both three-foot putts and probably easily made both. Regardless of the score value, a quintuple bogey or birdie, the same routine needs to be applied.

The Routine

Consistency is created. The magic formula for creating consistency is following the same proven routine for each putt attempt, in practice, during a pregame warm-up, and on the golf course during play. A solid routine on the golf course will create consistency, foster confidence, assure that all factors are accounted for, help to avert unforced errors, and lower your average number of putts per hole and per round.

All tour players have routines. Among the players, the routines are rarely exactly the same. What is the same, though, is that every good player has a consistent routine that he or she follows for each and every putt attempt, regardless of the circumstance and regardless of the value placed on the putt, whether it be for a double bogey or an eagle.

Here is how to develop your own routine for creating consistency. A great routine for the golf course is actually six separate routines combined into one. You will need to have solid habits for each part and then combine them all. The six parts of a great putting routine are:

- ► Before-the-round information
- ► Reading the green
- ► Rehearsal
- ► Preshot routine

► The stroke
► Post-putt analysis

Before-the-Round Information.   Ask the professionals at the course about the green speeds that day. Some courses will even post the green speed of the day on a signboard. At the practice putting green, begin your warm-up with a number of successful three-foot putts (five, ten, fifty, or a hundred) to align yourself to straightness. Continue your warm-up with a number of six-foot putts, 10-footers, and 20-footers to get a feel for the green's speed at distance. Finish your warm-up by playing a few putting holes from varying distances to get a feel for how the greens are being read and for applying your thoughts of the day, as well as for starting the day with confidence.

Reading the Green.   As you approach each green throughout the round and before you step foot onto the green, begin reading. (See Figure 3.1.) There is a lot of information to gain, so there is no reason to wait to be near your ball before you get started. You will want to apply your green-reading skills to determine the expected path of the putt and the distance needed.

We'll go into the finer points of green reading and apply them to a more detailed routine in Chapter 5, but in regard to consistency, here is a sample routine covering the basics of the basics. As you approach the green, look for major influences, such as surrounding terrain, hills and valleys, and so on. As you approach your ball to mark it, get a first impression of the breaks, both up- and downhill: left, right, straight, or double breaks. As you wait your turn to play, start confirming or debunking your first impression by reading the variables. Start from behind your ball, and then reconfirm the read from the opposite side of the hole. (See Figure 3.2.) When it is your turn to play, replace your ball and then read from behind the ball to ideally make a decision on the break. If you still have questions at this point, you need to reread from behind the ball, the opposite side of the hole, and both sides.

3.1. Great putters begin reading the green before they even stand on the putting surface.

After the reread, make your decisions. Before addressing the ball, from behind the ball, make your final decision on the break and see the intended line. Then determine the distance of the putt, accounting for any up- or downhill variables. When all of the variables are solved and a direction and distance are finalized, then the reading of the green is complete.

Rehearsal. A rehearsal is a practice swing designed to combine the knowledge that you have gained from reading the green with your motion and swing thoughts, so that you gain a feel and visual for the upcoming putt. (See Figure 3.3.) Some players stand behind the ball, facing the hole, while they rehearse the stroke. They look at the hole while they practice the stroke to combine their feel of the stroke with the visual image of their expected putt path. Other players stand astride the ball, while they try to perfectly emulate the stroke they

3.2. If you do not have a caddie to consult, you will have to spend a little extra time viewing the putt from other positions around the hole.

3.3. Once the player has decided on the read of the green, a rehearsal is used to assemble all of the information into a visual image of the upcoming hole out.

plan to use. No matter the style of rehearsal, you must use the same rehearsal for each and every putt. The rehearsal should last until you have gained the confidence that you are prepared to putt.

Preshot Routine.   Following the rehearsal is your preshot routine. Once you have gained confidence from your rehearsal and are sure of the proper path and distance after reading the green, you are ready to strike the putt. A preshot routine will always consist of the same elements and should always take the same amount of time. If your preshot routine becomes interrupted, you start over from its beginning. A great preshot routine will incorporate the following: a clear focus on the path, distance, and hole; solid and proper setup positions with relaxed muscles; and a mind fixated on positive results.

A good sample preshot routine begins with you standing maybe four or five feet behind the ball, taking a last look at the path you are about to make your ball follow. (See Figure 3.4.) As I mentioned while describing our 15-footer, I recommend picking a spot on that line about two or three feet ahead of the ball upon which to focus your aim. (You might choose a blemish, an old ball mark, a leaf, or debris of some kind.) Now address the ball by first placing the putter head squarely behind the ball; then place your feet and body in the correct alignment positions; next, grip the putter grip and make sure your arms are in the correct positions; and finally,

3.4. A good routine will be exactly the same for every putt attempt.

take your stance, making sure that you are comfortably in all of the correct preswing positions. Look at the hole, see your line or spot, and confirm that your putter's aim is on your intended line. Once you have confirmed the aim, look at the hole to see as well as feel the distance. Confirm your confidence in the distance. Look at the ball and take a relaxing breath. The preshot routine is over.

The Stroke. Immediately following the preshot routine, you begin the stroke. If all of your prior routines were successful, the stroke will be nearly automatic. The stroke only requires three elements: the start, the swing, and the finish.

All good putting strokes begin with a trigger. This is a tension-relieving signal that the stroke is about to begin. The trigger is any motion or action that is not the actual stroke but that enables the

3.5. Every great putter uses some form of a pendulum-type motion. A good pendulum will help to keep a rhythm and promote great distance control.

stroke to begin with ease and without the muscles overtensing. Any type of trigger will work as long as it accomplishes a tension-free, smooth transition into the stroke. Some proven triggers include a forward press of the hands, a slight lift of the putter, a hard look at the ball, a tap of the putter's sole lightly on the green as soon as a comfortable grip is achieved, or a knee press, which is usually the rear knee moving a few inches toward the hole.

The swing needs to be on autopilot, which will allow your sense of feel to re-create exactly the motion you have rehearsed (see Figure 3.5). If your mind is cluttered, your sense of feel will be interfered with and your chances of success greatly diminished.

The finish will need to be the same for each and every putt. By consistently finishing in the same manner, you create a comfortable and consistent stopping point for your body motion. (See Figure 3.6.) The most common method of making the finish routine is holding the body and putter positions steady until the ball is well under way—when the ball has gone at least five feet. This accomplishes three goals: a consistent and repeatable finish, an exact moment of completion of the stroke, and the ability to derive feedback for errant strokes. One more finishing thought is to follow the roll of the ball with the putter head until the putter is pointing at the hole.

Post-Putt Analysis. When the ball comes to rest at the conclusion of a putt, you will need to have a routine analysis to assess the success or failure of the putt. By analyzing the putt instantly, you will gain the necessary feedback to positively continue forward into another putt. The feedback you are after will help you to determine how to

3.6. Holding the finish is another important part of a routine. It shows the result of a smooth stroke.

proceed in the future. You will want to analyze the success of your direction and distance control, mental skills, and green reading. If the ball goes into the hole, your analysis will be quite simple and will lead only to a reinforced confidence that your methods are working. If the ball misses the hole, you will need to determine why, so you do not make the same error again, especially because the comeback putt will be on a very similar line to that of the putt just missed. Remember, just because you missed the putt, you should not simply assume that the mechanics were to blame. Most amateurs blame their mechanics first when there can be other reasons as well, like a mis-read, so do your post-putt analysis. Once you find the right routine for your putting game, you will have created consistency and will have given yourself one of the four basic skills necessary to mastering your putting game.

chapter

4

THE BASICS: PHYSICAL SKILLS

This is where the game of golf turns from a mental exercise into a physical activity. Having strong mental skills or consistent routines will contribute to your overall putting mastery, but when you arrive on the putting green to face a 20-foot putt, neither will matter unless you have the proper physical skills. By proper I mean that you are conditioned sufficiently to make the putter create a putting motion that sends the ball in the correct direction with the correct control of distance. There are two major elements to the physical requirements of successful putting. You need to control the distance of your putts and you need to start the putt in the correct direction. If you think about it, these two elements actually make the objectives of the putting game attainable. The objectives we defined in Chapter 1 are making the ball roll a specific distance and having it roll along a selected path.

When you master the distance-control skill, you will make more putts from greater distances and you assure yourself of no more than two putts per green. Controlling distance is a combination of being technically sound, being able to read greens, being able to gauge the exact distance to the hole, and having a feel for the amount of energy

47

necessary to impart to the ball to make it roll that particular distance. If you can learn to control the roll of all of your putt attempts to a distance that falls somewhere between the back of the hole and no more than 18 inches beyond it, you will have mastered the distance-control skill.

Being able to start the ball straight is what controls direction and allows you to complete the hole. Putting straight requires more intellectual ability than physical ability. I figure it takes as much physical ability to make a ball start straight as it does to open a sliding glass door. If you can repeatedly putt a ball on a level surface, perfectly straight along a line for three feet, you will have mastered this skill.

THE PUTTING LAWS

So far I have made it sound as if learning to master the physical skills is going to be as easy as a tap-in. If mastering the skills were this easy, we would all be on TV every weekend playing for big trophies. There are only two physical skills to master, but to do so requires that you obey the five putting laws, which will ultimately dictate whether or not you have success controlling distance and direction. As is the case with most laws, breaking them is bad and will get you in trouble. If you follow the laws, you will be a good putting citizen. The putting laws are:

1. Create a repeating swing path.
2. Maintain a square putter face at impact.
3. Connect the ball with the sweet spot.
4. Control the angle of attack.
5. Follow the club head speed formula.

Law #1: Create a Repeating Swing Path

Every time you swing a putter, it will create a path. Your job in creating a great putt is to create a path that will be most effective in sending the ball in the correct direction. The swing path is the path that the putter head follows during a putting stroke, on the back stroke, the through stroke, and into the follow-through. The perfect swing path is the one that travels along the ball's intended line of flight through impact. The importance of the swing path to putting straight is that, for the most consistently straight putt, time after time, the mass of the putter head needs to be moving in the exact direction that you want your ball to travel at impact. A faulty swing path, even with a perfect face position at impact, will start the roll of the ball on an unintended line (not in the right direction) or will put a sidespin on the ball. Both errors can cause the ball to roll off of the intended straight line.

The two paths I teach are straight-back straight-through (SBST) and inside-square-inside (ISI). (See Figures 4.1 and 4.2.) There are other paths, like inside to straight through, inside to outside, and outside to inside, but if you stick to one of the first two, your stroke will be much simpler to repeat. The SBST path is most accurate for direction and making short putts. The ISI path is good for feeling distance control on longer putts. You will want your putting stroke style (which we'll discuss in detail in Chapter 6) to fit with your swing path pattern.

Law #2: Maintain a Square Putter Face at Impact

The angle between the putter face and the intended straight line should be 90 degrees at the putter's impact with the ball. This 90-degree angle is also known in golf terms as square. (See Figure 4.3.) The importance of a square putter face to putting straight is that when you make a putt, the ball will deflect off of the putter face in the general direction that the putter face is directed. If you want a straight putt, the putter face must be perpendicular to the intended straight line. A faulty putter face position will cause the ball to immediately lose the intended straight line. A lot of the preswing mechanic positions have influence over the putter face position at impact.

4.1. Notice the differences between this back stroke and the one in Figure 4.2. A straight-back straight-through swing path creates a back stroke that is still in line with the ball and hole.

4.2. The inside-square-inside (ISI) is more to the inside of the putting line.

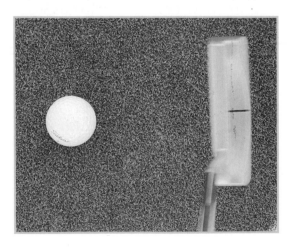

4.3. The face needs to be perfectly square to the intended starting line in order to deflect the ball in the correct direction.

Law #3: Connect the Ball with the Sweet Spot

In proper golf science terminology, the sweet spot is known as the centeredness of contact. It is a very exact spot within the putter head where energy is most efficiently transferred from putter to ball. Every putter and every ball has a sweet spot. Because the ball is an orb, the sweet spot is found on its equator. Most manufacturers use a line or dot to indicate the exact location of the putter's sweet spot. Some companies do not mark the spot, and others may actually mark the incorrect location. If you do not hit the sweet spot, you are not transferring energy efficiently and solidly, which results in all kinds of ways to miss a putt. The sweet spot is as tiny as a pinhead. This means that your mechanics must be efficient enough during the motion to return this pinhead into the back of the golf ball every time that you make a stroke. It is a good idea to check for yourself and make sure you know exactly where it is on your putter. (See Figure 4.4.)

Hold the putter lightly in your fingers about a foot above the club head on the shaft. Poke the point of a tee onto the putter face where you think the sweet spot should be. If the putter does not twist, then you have hit the sweet spot, or you have held the putter shaft too tightly. If the putter twists, this indicates that you have missed the sweet spot one way or another. Try again poking in a new spot, based on the twist of your miss. Once you find the spot, poke several more times to make sure it is correct. Once you are confident in the location, see if your putter's indicator is marked correctly. If it is not or your putter does not have an indicator, then

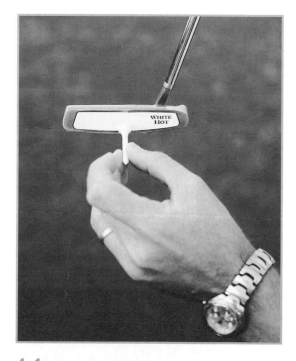

4.4. Use the sweet spot check technique to make sure you know where the actual sweet spot is on your putter.

put a dab of nail polish on the top of the putter so you will always know the exact location of the sweet spot. If you cannot figure it out, seek a golf professional for assistance.

The importance of hitting the sweet spot of the ball with the sweet spot of the putter in regard to hitting straight is that the energy transfer needs to be in line. A missed sweet spot, even if all other factors are correct, will cause the ball to have incorrect rotation and a degree of sidespin, which will further cause the ball to roll off a straight line rather quickly. The sweet spot is just as important for controlling your distance as it is for putting straight. By hitting the sweet spot of the ball with the sweet spot of the putter, you transfer all of the energy created with the motion of the putter into the ball. The farther you are from the sweet spot, the less effective the transfer of energy, which means it is more difficult to consistently control your distance.

Law #4: Control the Angle of Attack

The angle of attack is a golf science term that describes the vertical path and angle of the club head as it approaches and strikes the ball. If the angle is too steep, the ball will be hit into the ground, causing energy to be lost and the distance of the putt to be reduced, because the ball will be bouncing. If the angle of attack is too shallow, the sweet spot will be missed above the ball and again cause a lack of total energy transfer, a reduction in anticipated distance, and a bouncing ball. Controlling the angle of attack means having the club strike the ball as the club head moves parallel to the ground.

You can experiment for yourself in creating different angles of attack. Try making a putt with the putter never raised more than half an inch above the ground at any time during the stroke. This makes a very shallow angle of attack. Conversely, make a putt lifting the putter more than a foot in the air on the back stroke, and then striking the ball. This will create a steep angle of attack. The proper angle of attack for you will fall somewhere between those two, most likely closer to the more shallow angle.

Law #5: Follow the Club Head Speed Formula

The quick observation regarding club head speed is that the more speed generated at the moment of impact, the farther that the ball will travel, and conversely, the less club head speed, the shorter the traveling distance. (See Figure 4.5.) To obey the law you must also mind the other laws that affect distance control by finding the proper angle of attack and the sweet spot and then bringing everything together. I have a formula that is sure to improve your distance control by demonstrating how the three laws that affect distance work together to create a desirable shot. During the back stroke, your body creates potential energy. With the through stroke, you unleash that energy on a particular angle of attack and transfer that energy into the ball through the sweet spot. The formula is A + S + C = D (that is, angle

4.5. Club head speed is properly measured at the impact with the ball.

of attack + sweet spot + club head speed = distance control). To master distance control using the formula, you will need to master each of the separate laws. If you can ensure through practice that you get a repeatable angle of attack and consistent sweet spot contact, then the only variable that will change from one putt to the next is the club head speed. When this occurs, you simplify the formula to C = D (club head speed = distance). The slower the club head speed, the shorter the distance the ball will travel. Conversely, the faster the club head speed, the farther the distance the ball will travel. But to earn the right to use the simple formula, you must have mastered a consistent angle of attack and sweet spot hit.

THE BASIC MECHANICS

If you have any hope of being a good putting citizen and obeying the five putting laws, then you are going to need to understand the importance of the basic mechanics. Complex mechanics, like an overdose of medicine, can cause putting failure. A lot of players have struggled with their putting for so long that they have tried and/or incorporated hundreds of not-so-important mechanical ideas. For instance, I had a player tell me that he was trying to keep his right arm tight to his side while his left elbow was pointing toward the hole. He opened his stance but stood pigeon-toed because he was trying to get extra topspin on the ball to get it to roll more quickly off of the putter face. He came to me to figure out why he was having trouble making more putts. All of his unnecessary effort created complex mechanics and was the cause of his poor putting.

The best putters use a very simple set of basic mechanics. They let their subconscious handle the rest. Think about your particular mechanics of another physical skill. I wonder if you ever considered climbing stairs a skill. When you climb stairs, do you think about the angles of your knees and ankles or your spine angle as it relates to either eight- or ten-inch step heights? What about how much arm swing to apply and the pace and tempo of your stride? Have you ever thought when you got to the top, "I should have kept my head more steady"? I am going to guess that you have never thought about any of this. You simply have an unstated goal of climbing to the top, which you have practiced thousands of times before. You let your subconscious control the mechanics of climbing the stairs. You can absolutely learn a set of basic mechanics for putting, practice a thousand times, and turn your putting into a skill that will be just as easy to perform as climbing stairs. By the way, there are more mechanics involved in climbing stairs than in putting.

How basic is a basic set of mechanics? I think an easy analogy to compare with putting mechanics is the mechanics of an indoor power fan (a steady base, a motor or power source, a blade, and a rod to connect the blade to the power source). Aim the fan squarely in the direction you want the air to blow, and, well, there you have it. Creating an analogy is one thing; applying the reality of the human body's complexities to a simple fan is another. When I teach, I like to discuss the putting mechanics by focusing on individual body parts. If you break down the mechanics of each body part, it makes learning the mechanics easier, and you will learn to isolate your sensations to a particular area of the body. This will give you a better feel for your stroke and a better chance of sensing any incorrect mechanical movements. Each body part has preswing positions (which you review prior to every stroke) and motion mechanics that create the stroke.

Two components make up the one set of basic mechanics: the preswing component and the swing component. The rest of this chapter covers both components for each body segment.

Hands

The hands are what connect us to the putter, via the grip, and as they influence the putter face's position both before and during a putting stroke, it is essential that you use the hands properly. The hands also provide feedback and feel. When it comes to the hands and successful putting, there are no moving parts. If the fingers of the hands move, they create unwanted complexity. In our fan example, the hands would be the nut and bolt that connect the blade to the rod.

Mechanically, the best grip to use is the one that properly allows the face to be aligned during the preswing and then allows the putter face to return to the ball, during a stroke, to the exact position you had it at your preswing position. If the grip is not mechanically correct, the putter face may in the preswing be where you desire, but during the stroke, the poor mechanics will cause the putter face to change to a new position, causing a missed putt. Following are the basic mechanics

4.6. Here is an example of how the palms will be parallel to each other in the setup position of a left-hand low stroke.

for a good grip. (The hands have influence over all of the putting laws, so if you are struggling with your stroke, always check your hands first.)

The Preswing Mechanics of the Hands

▶ **Palm positions.** The palms should be in a position that allows the putter face to be positioned squarely, with proper grip pressure, and the grip to be held in a manner by the fingers that allows the putter shaft to be positioned at a proper angle. (See Figure 4.6.) Different strokes may require a variation in the palm positions.

▶ **Grip pressure.** A proper grip will need to be tension free with the correct amount of pressure from the preshot through the stroke until the ball is under way. To find the proper grip pressure, head to your bathroom and grab a new tube of toothpaste. Open the end and hold the tube as you would a putter grip. Now squeeze with both hands equally until the paste shows itself in the opening. If the paste comes squirting out, there's too much pressure; if it doesn't come out at all, there's not enough. You want to transfer this feel of pressure to your putter.

▶ **Hand positions.** For most strokes, the hands are positioned between the hips. To create a natural and tension-free position, you will need to keep your hands equidistant between the two hips (in the center). Some players use a hands forward of center position, which is acceptable for some strokes. Different types of strokes may require the hands to be positioned away from the center. (See Figures 4.7 and 4.8.)

The Swing Mechanics of the Hands

▶ **Consistent pressure.** Once you have created a comfortable grip pressure in the preswing, that same pressure needs to be used throughout the motion. A change in pressure during the stroke will cause

4.7. These images show the hands in two acceptable positions, the center of the stance . . .

4.8. and with a forward press.

misdirected putts. Tiger Woods says that the pressure he uses for putting on a scale of one to ten is a five. Ben Crenshaw uses a bit lighter pressure than that.

► **Hand rotation.** The proper rotation depends on whether you use a straight-back straight-through or inside-square-inside motion stroke. For a straight-back straight-through stroke, the hands will not rotate whatsoever. With a proper grip, the back of the forward hand faces the intended direction. Throughout the stroke, it will continue to face the same direction. For an inside-square-inside stroke, the hands as a unit will have slight rotation. The proper amount will vary from person to person, but it is very slight.

► **Path.** The palms will remain facing each other and should remain square to the putter face throughout the stroke. The path of the hands using the straight-back straight-through path moves them in a straight line; they should be swung back and forth exactly parallel to the straight line you want your ball to travel. Any deviation off of this line will cause a misdirected putt. For the inside-square-inside path, the hands will move slightly on an arc, a little shallower than the arc of the club head.

Arms

Mechanically, the arms are connecting rods. They connect the power source (shoulders) to the hands and putter. Just like the hands, the arms themselves will have no moving parts, despite the fact that they have two hinged joints (elbows and wrists). One of the greater challenges in the mechanics of putting is not allowing either of the joints to bend during the stroke. They need to remain in the same positions throughout the putt. The basics to good arm mechanics are that there is no joint movement and the arms should be swung by the power source (shoulders). For example, the arms during a putting stroke should move like the chains on a child's swing. The arms have the most influence over the laws of swing path, square clubface, and the sweet spot. If you have problems with one of these laws, then the arms might be the cause. The arms are the rod of a fan and also aid in alignment.

The Preswing Mechanics of the Arms. The arms are the connecting rods between the shoulders and the hands, and despite their two most obvious hinges, they should have no moving parts. The arms need to be set into proper positions to accomplish the basic mechanics and follow the laws. The preswing techniques of the arms are all about positioning.

► **Amount of bend.** The amount of bend for the arms will vary due to body type, posture, and stroke style. The less bend there is, with the ideal being straight with no bend, the easier it should be to maintain. Some players find that straight arms cause too much tension, so they add a little bend to relieve the tension. This is OK. The proper amount of bend for your arms will depend on your putting stroke. (See Figures 4.9 and 4.10.) The more the arms are bent, the more shoulder energy you will need to create distance. The straighter the arms are, the less shoulder energy you will need to create that same distance. Whatever amount of bend you use, you will need to re-create it for each and

4.9. Some players play with a lot of arm bend.

4.10. Others play with their arms much straighter.

4.11. Here is an example of how the elbows would be pointing straight away from the target when they are mostly bent.

every putt that you attempt and maintain the same amount of bend throughout the putt. The proper amount of bend will allow the putter head to be positioned under your eyes properly and allow the putter's sole to properly lie on the ground.

► **Elbow positions.** Where your elbows should point will depend on the amount of arm bend and your particular stroke. (See Figure 4.11.) If your arms are straight to slightly bent, the elbows will point to your hip bones. If you bend your arms a lot, heading to a 90-degree bend, the elbows will be pointing away from each other. If you draw a line between your elbows, this line needs to be parallel to your intended straight line.

► **Wrist angles.** The wrists can bend in two different directions: side to side and up and down. The best way to see the correct position is to let your arms hang at your side and look at your wrists' angles (by nature, there should be no angle). Having no created wrist angles is the best putting position for most strokes. There should not be any up-and-down angle, and the side-to-side angle with the arms straight should also be zero. As the elbows increase their bend, the side-to-side wrist angles will need to increase to match the bend. The less angle, the easier to repeat consistently.

► **Ball position.** The ball position toward and away from the hole is dictated by arm and wrist positions. The ball will need to be positioned in front of the putter's face, directly in line with the sweet spot, where the putter is moving level to the ground during the stroke. This is part of our arms discussion because the angles and bends of the arms and wrists will affect where the putter head will be in relation to the area

4.12. The ball position is different for different strokes. Make sure you determine where your putter swings level to the ground to find your ideal ball position. This is a traditional stroke ball position.

4.13. This is a good ball position for the belly putter stroke.

4.14. This is a split-hand stroke ball position.

between the hips. If you have straight arms and no wrist angles, then the putter head will be directly centered between the hips, which puts the ball in front of the putter and slightly forward of the center of the hips. Ball position can be slightly different for every person and each type of stroke. (See Figures 4.12, 4.13, and 4.14.) Once you find your ball position, it will always need to be the same.

The Swing Mechanics of the Arms

► **Joint movement.** Unnecessary movement will increase club head speed in regard to distance and can cause unwanted rotation of the hands, leading to missed putts.

► **Rotation.** The arms should not rotate during the stroke, so as to prevent joint movement while remaining tension free. The arms should remain parallel to your intended line throughout the stroke for most types of strokes.

▶ **Path.** The path that the arms follow is parallel to the intended line, just like all of the straight positions. Any deviation will cause sweet spot misses and distance-control loss. The arms should only be swung by the shoulders.

Body

Mechanically, the body is the foundation that keeps everything in balance and that supports the power source. Based on its positioning and alignment, the body influences the direction of a putt. Just like the hands and arms, the body during a putt will have no moving parts, even though the body has a lot of potential moving pieces. The body has more than 230 movable and semimovable joints. Wherever you position your feet, legs, hips, and torso at set-up, they still should be in the same positions during and throughout the stroke. The basics of good body mechanics are that there is no movement of the body and it must have proper alignment. The body has influence over the laws of swing path, square clubface, and the sweet spot. The body moving is the most problematic mechanic for a majority of players who have putting problems.

The Preswing Mechanics of the Body

We need to position the body in the preswing to help aim the stroke and to brace for no movement during the stroke. Just like the power fan, the body is to support the power source, and when positioned in a particular way, will send its energy in a particular direction.

▶ **Body position.** The body for distance control simply needs to remain motion free. The feet should be positioned away from each other at a certain distance to stabilize the entire body, create balance, and prevent movement. This varies from player to player. Some players position their feet to be nearly touching each other, while others position their feet in a stance wider than their shoulders. A basic position is that you place the insteps of your feet as wide apart as your shoulders. Personal modification is acceptable as long as it stabilizes the body and promotes balance. Your weight needs to be properly distributed between your feet. I prefer equal distribution between the feet. As long as the weight remains the same throughout the stroke, modifications of more weight on the forward foot are permitted. Some players do this to help stabilize their bodies. When positioning weight forward, though, modifications in shoulder tilt, hand positions, and ball positions need to happen because of the change in the angle of attack to a steeper angle. I would rather see you stay at fifty-fifty weight distribution. Hip tilt should not happen. Any tilt in the hips can only cause angle-of-attack problems.

▶ **Posture.** The posture of the body is determined by the amount of knee bend and the angle of the spine. It is easier to find consistency in the knees, as it is for the elbows, if they are kept straight. To relieve tension, a slight knee bend is common. Too much knee bend can cause some issues, so it is not recommended. The spine angle will vary from player to player due to body type, stroke, putter length, and health. The basic angle for a traditional stroke can be found by slightly bending your knees, allowing your arms to hang freely at your side, and then bending forward at the waist until your arms are hanging freely in front of you about six or eight inches from your thighs. (See Figure 4.15.)

4.15. Posture will vary among the putting strokes. This is a good posture for a traditional straight-back straight-through stroke.

▶ **Alignment.** Body alignment is the same as alignment of the arms and shoulders, parallel to the intended line. Draw lines between your heels, knees, and hips. They all should be parallel to each other for most strokes.

► **Tension.** Tension in the body can be tricky. Because we want no movement from the body, a little tension in the correct areas is all right. Leg and hip tension, just enough to keep these body pieces movement free, is acceptable. If their tension resonates throughout the rest of you, then it is too much, but if it stays local, it's OK.

► **Ball position.** The ball position to and away from you will be dictated by your body positions. The ball needs to be positioned directly under your eyes. So the ball position is based on your posture and body positions.

► **Eyes.** I like to include the eyes under the body heading. Mechanically, the purpose of the eyes is to prepare for the putt by properly positioning the player to the ball and the hole. Keeping the eyes level to the ground with the dominant eye over the ball will give you the best perspective to see the intended line of the putt. (See Figure 4.16.) Once a player begins the putting motion, the eyes have no mechanical function. In other words, do not let your eyes help you to make a complex putting motion. (No peeking.)

4.16. Here I am placing my dominant right eye directly over the ball.

The Swing Mechanics of the Body

The body is positioned in a manner that will prevent body motion and allows for consistent support for shoulder motion.

► **No movement.** There should be no body motion throughout a putting stroke. Any motion will cause directional errors. Any movement of the body affects the distance-control formula, which can cause great inconsistency.

Shoulders

Mechanically, the shoulders in a putt should be the sole power source for almost all the types of strokes. The shoulders are like the motor of a fan. Their motion swings the arms, hands, and putter, which creates the energy to move the ball. The method you choose to move the shoulders will need to accomplish the following:

► The ability to vary the power to control distance
► The ability to move the shoulders without any unnecessary movement from the body
► The ability to control the direction of the movement, which allows the putter to swing on a repeatable path

The basic principles of good shoulder mechanics are that the shoulders are positioned and maintained perpendicular, throughout the putting motion, to the path that you desire the ball to travel and they move in a rhythmic rocking motion. Because of their important job within putting, the shoulders have influence over all of the laws. Most players, due to their lack of understanding as to what the shoulders should be doing, tend to use the shoulders improperly if they use them at all. A lot of players learn to swing with just their arms, their shoulders frozen in place. The shoulders need to move if you want to make a lot of putts.

The Preswing Mechanics of the Shoulders

We need to prepare the shoulders in the preswing to allow them to most effectively accomplish the basics of the putting mechanics.

► **Alignment.** The shoulders are aligned the same as the arms. A line drawn from shoulder to shoulder is parallel to the intended straight-line direction of the putt for most strokes. Some strokes will require

4.17. Notice the slight bit of tilt in the shoulders, which is caused by the right hand being positioned lower than the left.

modifications to alignment. Whatever the alignment, it always needs to be the same for each and every putt attempt.

▶ **Tilt.** The shoulders will normally have some tilt. With one hand lower on the putter grip than the other, a relaxed shoulder will lower as much as the hand has lowered. (See Figure 4.17.) There is no need to exaggerate this tilt. The tilt will increase the farther the hands are positioned toward the forward hip. The greater the tilt, the steeper the angle of attack. With a steeper attack angle, you can run into distance-control problems.

▶ **Tension.** The shoulders need to be tension free. If the shoulders are fighting gravity, you have tension. Let your shoulders droop and relax. This is the proper tension-free position. It is good to find any tension in your shoulders before you stroke a putt, because you still have time to relieve the tension.

The Swing Mechanics of the Shoulders

The shoulders will move in a rhythmic rocking motion. The length of the motion will dictate the club head speed and the amount of energy transferred into the ball; it is the most important variable to the distance formula. The less that the shoulders rock, the shorter the roll of the ball, and the more they rock, the farther the rolling distance. Many golf instructors correctly create a visual image of this shoulder motion by saying that it looks like the swinging pendulum of a clock.

▶ **Rocking.** The amount and speed of the rock will create club head speed and will translate into the distance the ball will travel. The shoulders create a pendulum-type motion with the arms. For consistent distance control, the same rhythm and speed need to be used throughout the stroke. If the putter accelerates too quickly on the back stroke and then decelerates on the through stroke, the distance will be uncontrollable. By using the same rhythm and speed, the only variable that will change will be the length of the rock. The shorter the rocking with the same rhythm and speed, the less club head speed. The longer the rocking, the greater the speed. If the brain is allowed to calculate only a single variable, it can more quickly learn a feel for consistent distance control. To create the proper rocking motion, on the back stroke, the forward shoulder goes down and the rear shoulder will move up an equal amount. (See Figures 4.18 and 4.19.) The down stroke will be just the opposite.

4.18 and **4.19.** Here is a traditional stroke showing how the shoulders rock from the back stroke to the follow-through.

4.20. Shoulders, hips, knees, and toes will be parallel to the intended line throughout a traditional stroke.

► **Rotation.** The shoulders should not rotate for most strokes. They should remain square to your intended line. This is where I should introduce the notion of a pivot point within the motion of the swing. A pivot point is a point in the body that represents the uppermost portion of the swing. Think of a clock pendulum. The pivot point of that pendulum is at the top where it is attached to the clock mechanism. For most properly executed traditional strokes, the pivot point will be located between the shoulders in the neck or collarbone area. For other strokes, the pivot point may be located elsewhere. Knowing where the pivot point is within your stroke will allow you to execute the best possible pendulum motion. If there is shoulder rotation that causes the pivot to move, the putt will likely be missed.

► **Tension.** The shoulders need to remain tension free throughout the stroke with the same degree from shot to shot. If the tension changes during a stroke, distance control is lost. If tension changes from one stroke to another or from day to day, a different feel for distance control is needed. Be consistent and use the same amount of tension all of the time.

► **Alignment.** The alignment of the shoulders is square to the line of intended flight for most strokes. (See Figure 4.20.) They will remain in this position throughout the stroke and will not have any rotation.

chapter

5

THE BASICS:
GREEN-READING SKILLS

If your strategy is to always aim at the hole and hope it goes in, then while I applaud you for having a strategy, I hope you learn quickly that this will not be a winning one. Instead, take a close look at the green's contour and figure out how the nature of the green is going to move the ball. Green reading is the fourth necessary skill of putting. I define reading a green this way. It is the act of perceiving how nature's laws will affect the roll of an upcoming putt and then, based on those natural laws, deciding the most probable path that the ball will have to follow from its present location to find the bottom of the hole.

Even if your equipment is not perfect and you have yet to master your other putting skills, by simply reading the greens properly, you will dramatically increase your chances of holing more putts. Consider this scenario. Your putter is perfect—custom fit from the best manufacturer. You were blessed with the best skills imaginable, but you have no idea how to read a green. Every once in a while, strictly by chance, you happen to hit the ball on the proper line and it amazingly goes in. I would guess that, with these abilities but without much mathematical study, you could get the line correct in maybe one of fifty attempts on putts longer than six feet in length. Now for the importance of reading properly. With just average equipment and an average skill level but possessing the knowledge and ability to read greens perfectly, your odds could become as good as one in six on putts longer than six feet. The reason for this is because your faulty putter and shaky skills will still work successfully every so often because of compensations from your body's mechanics during the swing. Not being able to read the green will hardly ever work, unless it is a dead straight putt.

As stated earlier, the object of playing golf is to get the ball to go a particular distance and direction, which will result in it finding the bottom of the hole in the fewest attempts. Because it is unusual to hole out from off the putting green, even for the best players, putting is the part of the game where the ball is finally put into the hole. Because in putting, the ball remains on the ground, the particular distance and direction are not likely to be a straight line. So in order to putt the ball into the hole, you need to determine, by reading the green properly, what the line and path of the putt will be. If you have understood the definitions and explanations of reading a green, you know that it is not a physical exercise but a mental one.

GREEN-READING VARIABLES

To master green reading means that you are able to know exactly, prior to stroking the putt, the path the ball must travel to end up in the hole. It also requires that you gain an intimate knowledge of the variables involved, and the effects those variables cause on a rolling ball, and you must be able to apply that knowledge to a routine and use that routine for each and every putt. Each variable you learn will increase your chances of success. I have determined that there are forty-eight variables to consider and each one can cause a different effect on a rolling ball. By learning these variables and how each of them can affect a putt, regardless of your skill level or the quality of your equipment, your putting success will improve, and you will hole more putts.

So how exactly is a green read? A green is read by using your sense of vision to see the possible variables, using your sense of feel to sense changes in elevation, and then using green reading knowledge to interpret the possible variables to determine the path of the upcoming putt. Reading a green with precision involves understanding all of the many variables and how they affect a rolling ball, using a method to apply your knowledge of the variables to a putt, and applying all of this into a routine to create consistency in your reading greens on the golf course and throughout a round.

Of the forty-eight variables, some will affect your putting more often than will others. But at some time in your putting life, you will be faced with most of them. Following is a list of my forty-eight variables (falling under the categories of grass, time of day or year, weather conditions, surrounding terrain, course design, course damage, and maintenance issues), with discussion on whether they affect the direction of a putt, the distance of a putt, or both.

Grass

There are basically five types of grasses with their cultivars that are commonly used for putting surfaces: bent, Bermuda, poa, zoysia, and paspallum. Each one grows differently and will affect both distance and direction differently.

Grass blade width will affect both distance and direction. The thinner the blade width, the smoother the roll, the more likely the ball will roll on a true line, and the easier it is to control distance. The thicker the blade width, the bumpier the green will be, which makes it more difficult for the ball to roll on a true line and harder to control distance.

Grass color will affect both distance and direction. Color can indicate hills and valleys and depends on the angle of the sun. Different grass colors can also mean different varieties of grass growing in the same green. Colors can also show grass health issues.

Growing patterns will affect both distance and direction. Bermuda grass and paspallum grow by spreading themselves with runners across the ground, which will then root. The rest of the grasses grow in clumps. Grass with runners generally cannot be mown as closely as clumping grasses. It also creates a grain by having its blades lie more on their sides than straight up and down as the other grasses do. Grain is how the grass lies on the ground. A lot of players playing on Bermuda grass for the first time have great trouble reading the greens. This is because of the grain that this type of grass has. The players are just not used to how the grain affects the roll of the ball. With Bermuda the grass lies on its side. When a putt rolls into the lying blades, the ball will slow more quickly. When a putt rolls in the direction of the lying blades, the ball will roll with less friction and take longer to come to a stop. Putting across the grain, even on a perfectly level green, will cause the ball to actually curve in the direction that the blades are lying.

The number of blades will affect distance. The greater number of blades on a green, the more friction there will be, causing a slower roll than on a green with fewer blades. The number of blades can be varied with maintenance practices and grass health.

Grass heights will affect distance. The higher the grass height, the slower the ball will roll on the green. The lower the grass height, the faster the ball will roll. The different types of grasses will vary in height based on maintenance practices, the time of the year, and the health of the grass. During the best growing season, healthy grass can be maintained at its lowest possible height. During times of poor growing conditions, the grasses can be maintained at an increased height to help them remain healthy.

Grass age will affect both distance and direction. Newly sodded, sprigged, or seeded greens will be bumpy and inconsistent. As the grass matures with proper maintenance practices, the greens will smooth out. As grass ages, it can begin to mutate, and varieties not designed for greens, growing in the fairways or roughs, can encroach on the green, which will make the greens more inconsistent.

Time of Day or Year

Time of day will mainly affect the distance, but direction could also possibly be affected. The time of day has many different effects on a putt, whether it is morning issues of dew or frost, the maintenance crew not having mowed all of the greens, or the early morning sun angles. As the day progresses, new issues will arise. Dew and frost burn off, the grass grows, and course traffic increases. As the end of the day comes, increased grass heights (due to growth), increased course traffic, and low sun angles will all affect the putt.

Time of year will mainly affect distance, but direction could also be affected. The time of year will dictate the health of the grass, maintenance practices, falling leaves, birds, animals, insects, ground firmness, and the grass type (winter or summer grasses). The health of the grass varies throughout the year. During the stress of a hot summer, the grass can suffer, which, depending on how the superintendent tries to save the grass, can mean either dry and faster greens or more damp and longer blades, causing slower greens. Different insects affect greens at different times of the year. Earthworms can leave tiny little sand mounds across the greens, making for a bumpy and slower green. Greens infected with nematodes or mole crickets will have less grass, which can mean fast and bumpy conditions. Green firmness will definitely depend on the time of year. You can expect hard and fast greens during the winter in the north but slower and softer greens during the rainy spring season.

Weather Conditions

Wind will affect both direction and distance just a little. If it's strong enough, the wind can blow the ball off-line. Wind mainly affects the health of the green. Wind tends to dry out a green, which can make the surface roll faster than usual.

Rain mainly affects distance. The more water that is hitting the green, the slower the green will roll. If the rain is coming down hard enough, puddling will occur in low spots, which will most certainly slow a ball's roll. If you must play in hail, then not only will distance and direction be affected but your physical well-being also likely will be affected. If there are hailstones on the green, you can imagine how they would affect a putt. Snow will definitely affect distance and most likely will affect direction. The deeper the snow, the less putting that can actually be accomplished.

Dry conditions will affect distance. The drier the conditions, the more stress the grass will feel, which affects its health. Either you will face dry, faster putting conditions or, if the grass is being maintained properly, you will face dry on one green and wet on the next because the maintenance crew is doing its best to keep the greens from burning up through watering.

Wet conditions will affect both distance and direction. The wetter the greens are, the slower they will roll. Wet greens make it difficult to properly mow on schedule, and even if mown, the softer ground will create more friction. The longer the greens are wet, the more probable that footprints and damage will occur, thus causing more issues.

Cold conditions will affect both distance and direction. The colder the air and ground are, the less the grass is growing and the harder the ground, which means the greens will roll a little faster. The longer the grass goes without healthy growth, the more damage will occur and the thinner the grass will become.

Hot conditions will mainly affect distance, with different results depending on the variety of grass. The hotter the air is, the faster the greens will grow (in the case of Bermuda and paspallum) or the more stress the grass will face (true for the other grasses).

Surrounding Terrain

Mountains will affect both distance and direction. Nearby mountains will affect how the green will lie. The more mature the green, the more that the mountains' slope will have an effect. Newer greens can actually be built against the slope of a mountain, because of the designer's understanding that over time the green will shift due to gravity and erosion. Greens on the side of mountains also usually drain very well, causing a drier green and a faster roll.

Hills have the same effect as mountains but with fewer dramatic changes over time. Valleys will mainly affect distance. Greens in a valley will be generally sloped by the course designer. A valley green may have some drainage issues during wet periods, which can cause slower rolling speeds. Open fields allow the wind to blow a little harder, which may dry out the greens, making them a little faster.

Woods will mainly affect distance. Greens in the woods are shielded from wind, which allows moisture to remain longer and, in hot periods, allows the sun to more intensely heat the green. If not maintained properly, greens in the woods have a greater chance of health issues. Trees will mainly affect distance. Trees that are in close proximity to the green can cause weaker growth of the greens by not allowing in a sufficient amount of sunshine. This can cause the grass to be thinner and roll faster.

Ponds will mainly affect direction. Rain and sprinkler water will generally drain toward the pond. This drainage can cause erosion, making the green slope more favorably toward the pond. Lakes have the same effects as ponds. Seas have the same effects as ponds and lakes, with the added problem of salt intrusions and a greater chance of increased winds. Most grasses do not like the salt, and if they are not maintained properly, the health of the grasses can be greatly tested.

Course Design

Green size does not directly affect distance or direction, but the larger a green is, the better chance you have of facing a long putt. The longer a putt is, the more variables there are to figure out. The smaller the green, the lesser the chance at a long putt, which means you will have fewer variables to figure out. Smaller greens also have traffic pattern issues. On a small green with a lot of play, more people have to walk in a smaller area, which means the health of the green can become an issue.

Green shape will mainly affect direction. The course designer determines the shape of a green; the more complex the shape, the more effort that was required in its creation because of the lay of the land, which can result in a more undulating putting surface. Think about a kidney-shaped putting green. You may be on a part of the green where it may be impossible to get a straight line to the hole because there is rough in between. If the green was designed well, there will be slope built in to allow the putt to bend around the rough. Most complexly shaped greens are not flat. They are complex because of the terrain. Designers are not looking to create impossible shots but to make for challenging shots that can be figured out if you know what to look for. Look for slopes the designer has used to accommodate the intricate shapes.

Bumps mainly affect direction but can influence distance. The larger the bumps are, the greater the influence on the roll of a putt.

Bumps, because of their nature, tend to deflect the ball off their sides. Unless your putt is directly over the apex of the bump, it will deflect one way or the other.

Hills in the green affect both direction and distance. The larger the hill, the more gravity will affect the roll, in both the speed the ball travels and the degree of break. The angle that you are putting on the hill will affect the direction the ball will ultimately travel.

Depressions will mainly affect direction. These are also called bowls on the green. The direction the ball will travel depends on the angle through the bowl. Although the opposite of a bump, depressions have the same effects. Instead of up and over a bump, the ball is traveling down and up a depression.

Very similar to a hill, slopes will affect both direction and distance, except that a sloping green has no top. It will slope from one side to the other. Gravity is the full influence on a slope, and the degree of the slope will determine the amount of break and distance the ball will roll.

Drainage will affect mainly direction. Course designers need to take into account the drainage of both rain and sprinkler water. How a designer handles drainage can greatly influence how a green will roll. The path of the drainage will erode over time and can increase the degree of how the green lies.

Course Damage

Amount of play will affect both direction and distance. The more play that occurs on a green, the more health issues that will arise, and the more maintenance practices that will need to be applied.

Foot depressions will affect both direction and distance. Foot depressions cause a bumpy putting surface. Each depression will deflect a rolling ball in one direction or another, and the impending bounce will absorb some of the ball's energy, causing the ball to roll less.

Old holes will affect both direction and distance. Improperly maintained old holes will cause the same issues as foot depressions. The big difference is that the rules of golf allow us to repair damaged old holes. Pitch marks will affect both direction and distance. They are the same as foot depressions and old holes. As is true for old holes, the rules allow us to repair pitch marks as well.

Spike marks will affect both direction and distance. The rules do not allow us to repair spike marks. They will deflect a rolling ball, and if hit squarely, they can cause the ball to bounce, reducing its rolling distance.

Equipment damage from tires, oil or lubricant spills, and the cup setter for the holes will affect both direction and distance. You will encounter the same issues as with spike marks.

Maintenance Issues

Weeds will affect both direction and distance, the same as with spike marks, though maybe even more severely. Fungus will affect both direction and distance. Fungus can kill the grass, causing bare areas. These bare areas will cause deflections and bouncing. Some new areas of fungus will cause a thinning of the grass, which can actually make these areas roll more quickly.

Insects will affect both direction and distance. Insects can create mounds, which can cause deflections and bounces. Subterranean insects can weaken the health of the grass, causing thinning areas of grass, which can make the green roll faster. If they have done enough damage to create sandy areas with very little grass left, these areas can be slower.

Aeration holes will affect both direction and distance. This is a necessary maintenance practice to keep the grass roots healthy by reducing soil compaction. Playing on aerated greens has several issues, chief among them that the green will be full of quarter- to half-inch holes, each one capable of causing a deflection and/or bounce.

Verticutting lines will affect both direction and distance. This is a necessary practice, especially for grasses with runners, where the maintenance crew slices vertically into the soil. This creates little lines that run over the entire green from one side to the other. The lines are relatively thin, but they can cause deflection or bumps.

Top-dressing will affect mainly distance. This is a maintenance practice where the crew drops a light layer of sand onto the putting surface. This is done to smooth the green and fill in any depressions. Top-dressed greens, depending on the amount of sand, will affect the distance a ball will roll. The more sand, the less roll. The less sand, the more roll. With the appropriate amount of sand, the greens will be at least the same as if not faster than normal.

Rolled greens have an effect on distance. This is a maintenance practice where a heavy roller is rolled over the green to both smooth the surface and make the ground more firm. This practice will make the greens speedier.

Fertilizers and chemicals will affect direction and distance. Fertilizers are applied onto the surface of the green, which can make the green bumpy. If the fertilizer gets wet, it can also stick to the golf ball while it is rolling, causing all kinds of trouble. There are many types of chemical applications that can cause varying green-reading issues.

Birds and animals will affect both direction and distance. There are many types of birds and animals that can cause many varied problems to the green. Most issues involve deflections or bounces, but on the rare occasion, birds or animals might also leave something behind that adheres to the ball, causing not only distance problems but also ball-handling problems.

GREEN-READING ROUTINES

Learning each variable is just the beginning to reading the greens. Because there is no truly accurate formula that will dictate how much each variable will affect the direction and distance of a putt, you will have to rely on your own personal experience and memory to learn to judge the amount of distance and directional changes that each of the variables will create. Given that creating consistency is a necessary skill of golf as a whole and of putting specifically, putting consistency must also be achieved when it comes to reading the greens. To do that, you need a routine to organize your green-reading knowledge into a simple process to allow you to quickly determine the most probable path of a putt. This will become a part of your larger routine, discussed earlier. You could spend hours analyzing an upcoming putt if you painstakingly review each and every variable to its minutest detail. With a routine and some practice, you should be able to read a green effectively in very little time. The exact amount of time will depend on your routine. A great green reader begins studying the variables before the round begins and continues until the last putt is holed. The reason that reading a green should take very little time is that by the time you face a putt, you should have already learned the details of many of the variables, leaving only a handful remaining to decipher. The few variables left to solve will be found between the ball and the hole.

The routine you should use needs to be simple. First, gain as much information about the greens as you can before the round ever begins, so you do not waste time while you are on the course. Begin your green reading in the golf shop. Ask the local pro for the type of grass on the greens, the age of the greens, and whether there has been recent course maintenance, like verticutting, top-dressing, aeration, fertilizing, or rolling. Also ask the pro for the speed of the greens that day and if there were any weather occurrences that may affect the greens' speed. Having information on these issues will get you mentally prepared even before you hit the practice green.

Once you hit the practice green, you want to see how the greens look. Look for damage like worn-out areas, weeds or fungus, and the extent of foot depressions in the greens' surface. You want to hit some putts to get a feel for how they are rolling. Are they smooth or bumpy, fast or slow?

After the practice green, if you are on a new golf course, you want to look around to gain knowledge on the size of the greens and the surrounding terrain, as well as get a general feel for what the greens are going to throw at you today. A final look at the weather forecast for the time you will be playing will give you all the information you need before you begin your round.

Once the round begins, you are going to be reading the greens from all over the golf course. There are many locations to gain green-reading knowledge. Observe upcoming holes from the tee box and fairway, as you approach the green, as you enter the green, and on the green from all sides of the hole.

If you can see the green of an upcoming hole, you can gain information as to where the hole location is as well as on the general slope of the green and the surrounding terrain. This will give you a little advantage when you finally arrive at that green.

From the fairway, you want to observe the terrain surrounding the putting green. This will give you basic information as to the slope of the green on two sides of the hole. If there is water next to the green, you can learn about possible drainage directions, which will also give you slope information. Additionally, reading from the fairway can give you hints about green speed variations if the green is up in the wind or shaded by trees close to the putting surface.

As you approach the green, you will be seeking a little finer detail. Look closely at the green's hills and slopes, as well as the green's size and shape, bumps, and depressions. Think about the time of day and year and how they affect the greens throughout the round. Observe the weather for any changes. Has the wind picked up or a quick shower passed? Has the sprinkler system recently watered the green?

When you step onto the green, you should already have a basic sense of the general direction your upcoming putt should break. Now is when you will seek the details that separate your ball from the hole. Look for course damage, like old holes, ball marks, bird or animal damage, and equipment damage. You can also see the grass color, which will give you an idea about the health condition of the green and possibly the direction of the grass's grain.

From behind your ball, you can observe the final details concerning the direction of the putt. Look for the actual line where you intend to roll your ball. See if there are any bumps, depressions, hills, or slopes that will cause the line to be altered. Look for maintenance issues and course damage between your ball and the hole, and make the necessary target line adjustments.

At this point, you should have considered every possible variable that could affect the upcoming putt and be ready to play. If you have any misgivings, step back and review the intended line. If you need to move around the hole to seek any information that you may have missed during the routine, now is the time. Remember, more often than not, your original feeling of the intended line is usually correct. There are more players who miss putts because they do not trust their original read than there are players who make them by second-guessing themselves. Once you have a read, putt the ball with confidence.

Following the putt, if you happen to miss, observe the ball roll past the hole so you can see the actual break. It is easier to read the green when a ball is rolling along or close to the intended line than without the ball rolling. You may have missed the first putt because you misread one of the variables. The ball rolling past just might show you what you missed, so you do not do it a second time and cause a three-putt error. Whether you miss or make it, you want to walk away from the hole knowing which variables you read correctly and which you may have read incorrectly. You will need to use this information on future holes.

chapter

6

SEARCHING FOR
THE "PERFECT" STROKE

Believe it or not, there are probably as many ways to putt a ball as there are days of the year. I have two players at my club with putting strokes that hopefully will never be seen outside of their foursomes. Their strokes are incredibly unusual, but I must admit, they are very productive for those two players.

A HISTORY OF TRADITIONAL PUTTING

I have a theory on how putting strokes have evolved. What I feel is the oldest of the strokes, the traditional inside-square-inside stroke, is a stroke that has evolved directly from the full swing. Way back at the beginning of golf history, greens had yet to be invented. The areas around the holes, called either the hole green or the table land, were not kept any differently than the rest of the course. Also, there were no teeing grounds (tee boxes). Players were supposed to tee off within a club's length of the hole they had just finished. This made the table land rather bumpy and inconsistent—not very good for what we would call putting. Most players would finish the hole with a chip. (A chip shot is simply a smaller, shorter version of the full swing.)

The traditional *inside-square-inside stroke* is based on the body's natural movements. When golf began, there were no golf instructors and no in-depth studies of the mechanics of the physical motions of the golf swing. Players simply played and learned to play with whatever came naturally. In the beginning, because putting the ball into the hole involved a lot more luck than skill, the players who could create distance with full shots had a distinct advantage over the other players. So players learned to stand facing the ball with the target 90 degrees to their sides. This allowed the player to create torque, which allows the player to hit the ball farther. The method the players used to make the ball travel shorter distances was to naturally use less swing motion. They did not think that they should mechanically do everything differently just to make the ball cover less distance. Thus, when the putter blade was introduced after surfaces became consistent enough to allow a ball to roll, the easiest method to apply was to shorten up the chip swing and create the traditional inside-square-inside stroke.

As the game of golf aged, players evolved their games and techniques to give themselves an advantage over their competition. The areas around the holes became less bumpy, and by 1812 when the term *putting green* was first referenced in the *Rules of Golf*, players began to modify the putting stroke. Some players realized that with a surface capable of having a ball roll somewhat true, they could gain an advantage as they got closer to the hole. They determined that they would concentrate on keeping the path of the putter on a straight line both on the back stroke and through the putt instead of the arcing path of a normal swing. This would give them more control over the direction of the putt over shorter distances, thereby allowing them to make more putts than they had before. Previously, putters were just less lofted irons. Now designers could create putters that would accommodate the player's new stroke mechanics and help keep the putter *straight-*

back and straight-through. The traditional strokes, both straight-back straight-through and inside-square-inside, have been and still are the overwhelming choice of most players. I believe the reason for this is because the game has a very long tradition.

REBELS ON THE GREEN

I am sure that golfers were experimenting with different types of putting strokes throughout the ages, but none of history's greatest players altered from the traditional strokes. This was true until the great Sam Snead decided he needed a putting advantage and changed his stroke. In 1968 he started putting with the ball between his feet, with his body facing the hole, croquet style. He quickly won with this stroke, because on more manicured greens, complete accuracy control due to a perfect straight-back straight-through path and motion would provide a tremendous advantage. The greens were becoming good enough that skill now was far outweighing luck when it came to holing putts. The croquet stroke—much too different from the styles and traditions of golf—was quickly outlawed by the rules governing body. With the new rules in place, Sam Snead simply retooled the stroke by placing his feet together, still facing the hole, and then placing the ball at his side. The rules allowed this modification, and he continued to play and win money with this stroke for many years. He called this stroke the *sidesaddle*. (See Figure 6.1.) It always takes a brave pioneer to buck tradition and show the rest of us that there may just be a better way than the old tried and true.

6.1. Sam Snead with his sidesaddle putting stroke.

6.2. The long putter has allowed many players, such as Shingo Kata-yama, to putt with confidence.

It was not until many years after Sam Snead that another great player would attempt to win with a nontraditional putting stroke. The next big leap in putting came in 1985 when Charles Coody lengthened his putter, stood upright, and secured the top of the club to his chest. This created an anchor point for the putter. (See Figure 6.2.) This stroke again changed the way that players thought about putting. This change occurred at a time when putting greens were being transformed into smoother surfaces by advances in both maintenance techniques and the types of grasses being used. With these better greens, an emphasis was being put onto the skill of controlling direction. The *stand-up stroke* is unique because it was the first time a club was anchored during the stroke. Anchoring the putter creates a solid pivot point; in the traditional strokes, there is no attached pivot point. This anchored pivot point makes controlling the accuracy on shorter putts much easier. This stroke gives the players who use it instant confidence because of the simpler mechanics and the ease with which it can be learned. This stroke was quickly adopted by many golfers and to this day is one of the most widely used strokes for putting.

Because so many players made the switch to a long putter and this unique stroke, the minds of other players were opened to the idea of trying new putting strokes. Players realized that using a stroke just because tradition dictates is not necessarily the best option to holing more putts. While obeying the rules of golf, players have discovered putting strokes that are highly effective for their personal games. What the creators of these modern strokes have learned is that if you modify the putting stroke to cure a specific mechanical flaw and/or to have the putting stroke fit your natural instincts it does not matter what the stroke eventually looks like. It matters more how well the stroke putts the ball into the hole.

With the putting surfaces today becoming increasingly smooth and fast, players are in need of a putting stroke that allows them greater control over distance and direction. The better players learned that there are not just one stroke but many different strokes to make putts. As a result, in addition to the traditional inside-square-inside and straight-back straight-through strokes, as well as the innovative sidesaddle and stand-up putting strokes, several other new strokes like the belly putter stroke are being used today by some of the world's best players. (See Figure 6.3.)

The *split-hand stroke*, which was made famous by Natalie Gulbis, employs methods similar to those used by hockey players hitting a puck and baseball players bunting. (See Figure 6.4.) It provides the easiest way to control your mechanics and create a repeatable, controlled shot.

The *cross-handed stroke* was created as a cure for overactive wrists during a putt. As greens have become faster, players have learned that extra wrist movement causes missed putts. Reverse the positions of the hands from the traditional positions and you will instantly reduce the amount of wrist action. (See Figure 6.5.)

The *claw stroke* is another grip-altering stroke. (See Figure 6.6.) When you adjust your rear hand into a more natural position, similar to the position of the hand while playing a violin, your arm will react like a piston, which allows the putts to become more accurate.

The *belly putter stroke* is finding much success among many great players. They have found that by lengthening their putter slightly,

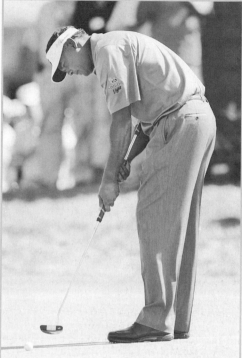

6.3. The belly putter stroke may not look traditional, but it certainly is effective for Vijay Singh in creating a solid stroke with an anchored pivot point.

6.4. This stroke looks more like hockey than a traditional putt, but players like Natalie Gulbis are finding it very easy to make effective.

6.5. Jim Furyk has played his whole golfing life with the cross-handed stroke.

6.6. The claw stroke of Chris Dimarco is one of the most unique putting strokes to have won on the PGA Tour.

anchoring it just above their belly button, and gripping midway down the shaft of the putter, they can eliminate a lot of extra, unwanted mechanical movements and allow the putter to be moved much more naturally. This stroke is a simple modification of the traditional inside-square-inside stroke.

EIGHT PUTTING STYLES

Choosing the right putting stroke is essential to becoming a better putter. By choosing the style that fits you, you will give yourself the best opportunity to create a consistent and repeatable motion, guaranteed to improve your putting results. I am going to show you each stroke and discuss its benefits, as well as what type of putter to use for each stroke. I will also detail the stroke-specific mechanics necessary to make the stroke successful. For consistency and ease of illustration, all of the strokes will be discussed for a player playing right-handed. Left-handed players need to apply the opposite positions to find success with the strokes.

Inside-Square-Inside

This is the original putting stroke, and it has a large presence out on the professional golf tours. This is a very traditional stroke. Approximately 95 percent of all tour pros use this stroke today. The contemporary version of the stroke is more subdued than the original. The old days of the stroke employed more wrist motion to create distance. On the old putting greens, due to their condition, it required more energy to send a ball a particular distance as compared to modern greens. Nowadays, with the greens as fast as they are, a 10-foot putt is like a four-foot putt of years ago. The inside-square-inside stroke is based on a natural body movement, which creates an arc. When you turn the shoulders on an inclined plane, there is no need for the hands or arms to rotate. When used correctly, the putter is always on a plane and the putter face is always square. It is a simple stroke with only one moving part. The mechanics are uncomplicated and allow for great feel. Ben Crenshaw, Raymond Floyd, Phil Mickelson, David Frost, Dana Quigley, Jerry Kelly, Arnold Palmer, K. J. Choi, Bobby Jones, Walter Hagen, Brad Faxon, and Bobby Locke have all successfully used the inside-square-inside stroke.

The Stroke's Theory.   The theory of this stroke is that by setting up in the traditional golf shot and athletic positions, moving the shoulders and nothing else, the club will travel an inside-square-inside arcing path. As stated, the path of this stroke is not a straight line but an arcing line. Imagine a perfectly level green. The intended line of the

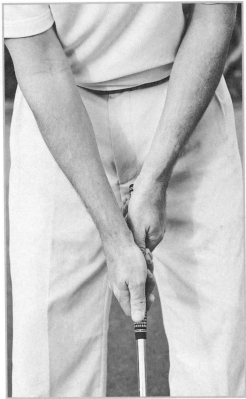

6.7. In this basic ten-finger grip, the palms face each other. A lot of players will overlap the pinkie of the lower hand over the forefinger of the top hand.

putt is a straight line toward the hole. An inside-square-inside path will have the putter move toward you a bit on the back stroke, return to a straight path toward the ball for about an inch or two, and then move toward you a bit again on the follow-through. By not manipulating the path, this stroke offers a great amount of consistency and feel, with a very simple set of mechanics. You can use any traditional-length putter in a blade or flange form for this stroke, providing the putter fits your swing path.

Grip the Putter. A basic grip is used, with the palms facing each other. (See Figure 6.7.) The grip is held more in the palm of the left hand than in the fingers. This will help position the shaft so that it is in line with the forearm. Create a gripping routine for ultimate success. A basic gripping routine for a traditional stroke is as follows:

1. Hold the putter shaft parallel to the ground with the toe of the putter pointing to the sky.
2. Position your forward hand first, along the finger lines with your thumb on top.
3. Slide the other hand into position.

Take Your Stance. The arms need to hang naturally, almost fully extended. The arms will create the letter Y position with the putter shaft, which will place the hands midway between the hips. The elbows will have only a slight bend to help reduce tension and should be pointing in the general direction of the hips. This will allow the arms to be properly swung by the shoulders. The hands will be positioned far enough away from the body to allow the club to swing freely without interference from the body, especially the rear thigh. The proper distance will depend on the particular spine angle in the posture. The correct position puts the hands at a slight angle outside the shoulders, not directly hanging under the shoulders as with some other strokes. The eyes will not be positioned directly over either but just slightly inside of the ball's position. This helps a person to see the arc path properly and assures that a good arc is created. (See Figure 6.8.) Remember to keep the eyes level. If the eyes are not level, the path of the arc will move in the wrong direction. The stance, including the feet, hips, and shoulders, needs to be square to the intended line. Any deviation here will cause a crooked arc path. The feet need to be balanced, front to back, heel to toe.

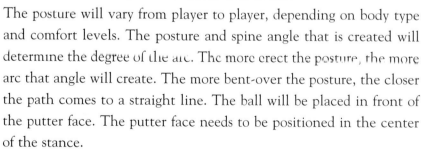

6.8. For an arcing path, the eyes should be positioned just on the inside of the ball instead of directly above.

The posture will vary from player to player, depending on body type and comfort levels. The posture and spine angle that is created will determine the degree of the arc. The more erect the posture, the more arc that angle will create. The more bent-over the posture, the closer the path comes to a straight line. The ball will be placed in front of the putter face. The putter face needs to be positioned in the center of the stance.

Stroke the Putt. The only moving parts of this stroke are the shoulders. They will move in a rocking motion. Hands, wrists, and arms must remain passive throughout the stroke. By not manipulating the hands and wrists, the putter face will rotate slightly, both on the back

6.9. Notice the rotation of the putter face and forearms. They should only rotate by means of the shoulders and should not be manipulated by excessive wrist action.

and through strokes. The amount of rotation will depend on the amount of arc your particular stroke makes. (See Figure 6.9.) The putter's face does not remain square to the intended target line but square to the path of the arc. Because the shoulders are moving them, the hands and arms will also move on an arc path. The degree of the arc will be less than that of the putter head and will feel almost as if the hands and arms are moving straight-back straight-through. This is because the degree of arc with the hands and arms is so minimal.

Straight-Back Straight-Through Stroke

This is what I call the first modification to the original putting stroke and is considered the second traditional stroke. The theory behind this stroke is that if the putter swings on the exact path that you want your ball to travel, the ball has a better chance of starting out in the intended direction with a good end-over-end roll of the ball. When this stroke is applied correctly, the putter stays on path, the putter face remains square, and it sends the ball in the exact direction you intend. If it were not for the set of mechanics required to create a perfectly straight path, every player would use this stroke. As it stands, it is the most popular stroke for amateurs to attempt. This is a small sample of the great players known to have played the straight-back straight-through stroke: Tiger Woods, Annika Sorenstam, Paula Creamer, George Archer, Ernie Els, Jack Nicklaus, Jay Haas, Bob Charles, Greg Norman, Loren Roberts, Dave Stockton, and Tom

Watson. Two young Florida pros to watch who also use this stroke are Brittany Lincicome and Kyle McCarthy.

The Stroke's Theory.   The theory behind the success of this stroke is that by achieving the correct setup positions, the putter will be moved by the shoulders alone, creating simple, reliable mechanics that move the putter on a straight-back straight-through path, which is the exact path that the ball should be traveling upon. The straight-back straight-through path is a straight line. Imagine a perfectly level putting green again. The intended line of a putt is straight at the hole. A straight-back straight-through path will have the sweet spot of the putter remain directly above the intended line at all times during the back stroke, down stroke, and follow-through, which also means that the putter moves directly away from and toward the hole. If the putter is moving along the intended path and the putter face remains square to that path, it will be awfully hard not to have the ball go in the correct direction. The most effective type of putter to use for this stroke is a mallet type, with face balanced, and, if you can be comfortable with the look, center shaft position in the club head. The bestselling putter ever, the two-ball putter, is beautifully designed for this stroke.

Grip the Putter.   A solid basic traditional grip is needed. You can use the same grip technique as described for the inside-square-inside stroke.

Take Your Stance.   Place your feet, hips, and shoulders parallel to the intended line. The ball position needs to be directly under the eyes and level to the ground. I recommend placing your dominant eye over the ball. Posture is the critical element for this stroke, and having the correct posture provides the easiest, most naturally effective method of making this stroke work. In order to have the path of the putter follow a straight-back straight-through path without difficult compensations, the posture cannot be erect. It must be bent to as close to 90 degrees as possible. If the posture is more upright, there are compensations that will still keep the path straight-back straight-through, but the compensations will require more practice and timing. The more upright the posture, the more natural movements the swing will create, resulting in an arc path with the putter head. Due to the amount of bend in the posture, the posture wants to force the weight toward the toes. The weight needs to be balanced evenly though, achieved by keeping the hips over the heels. The desired outcome is a good posture with the weight even from heel to toe and from forward to rear foot. The arms in this stroke will need to be bent to some degree to accommodate both the need to position the eyes directly over the ball and the exaggerated posture. Whatever the amount of wrist and arm bend is created in the setup, that amount of bend needs to remain the same throughout the stroke. Arms need to hang naturally from the shoulders, as if you let gravity hold them, so that the hands hang directly beneath the shoulders. Hold the putter shaft as vertical as possible. A perfect straight-back straight-through path can be created with a nearly vertical putter shaft position. The forearms need to be parallel to the intended target line. (See Figure 6.10.)

Stroke the Putt. The shoulders are the only required moving element of this stroke, and they should move in the basic rocking motion. The posture needs to remain in the exact angle it was placed in the setup throughout the stroke. To keep the putter face square, the hands and wrists need to remain passive, making sure to not allow any rotation. The hands and arms need to be moved by the shoulders alone. They will be moved along the straight-back straight-through path, the same as the club head. (See Figure 6.11.)

Cross-Handed Stroke

This putting stroke has been around for centuries, and as far as I can determine, it was created more as a practice drill to help solve excessive wrist movement than as a putting stroke with which to play

6.10. A solid set-up position, with the eyes over the ball, hands between the hips with an equal balance of weight, and a slight shoulder tilt.

6.11. This stroke is about keeping the club head moving along the intended line of putt, both back and forward. At the same time, the putter face remains square to the line.

championship golf. Jim Furyk is the first winning PGA Tour player to have grown up playing this stroke and use it throughout his golfing career. Jim's father taught this stroke to his son after asking Arnold Palmer and Gary Player what they would have done differently in their careers. Both answered that they would have putted cross-handed. With that answer, Mike Furyk taught his son the cross-handed stroke. Jim Furyk has been known as a great putter for a good many years. This stroke has been favored by many great professionals in addition to Furyk, including Arnold Palmer, Gary Player, Tom Kite, Bernhard

Langer, Fred Couples, Vijay Singh, Nick Faldo, Tom Kite, Jesper Parn-evik, Fred Couples, Tom Watson, Ernie Els, Julie Inkster, Karrie Webb, and Se Ri Pak.

The Stroke's Theory.   This stroke is designed to solve problems (specifically excessive wrist action) that are common within the two traditional strokes. When the unwanted wrist action occurs, it is nearly impossible for the putter to remain on the proper path consistently, causing a lot of missed putts. Switching the hand positions (with the left hand low on the grip and the right hand on top) takes away unwanted wrist action mechanically, without the need for manipulating swing thoughts or extra practice. This stroke causes the shoulders to be in a more level position at setup. The putter to use for this stroke can be any traditional-length putter. You can use either the straight-back straight-through path or the inside-square-inside path, so you will want to make sure the putter fits the swing path that you use for the stroke.

Grip the Putter. The grip is the main feature of this stroke. The hands are held with the palms facing each other, with the right hand being positioned at the top of the putter and the left hand being placed below the right and the back of the left hand positioned squarely with the putter face. Some players will extend the forefinger of the right hand down and on top of the fingers of the left hand. Due to the right hand being higher on the grip, the right arm has a bend, which will act as a piston. The left arm needs to hang naturally, and the forearm will align parallel with the putter shaft. Once the hands are on the grip, lean the club to your left so that the fingers on your right hand are pressed lightly against your left forearm. This will help lock the hands together so they work as a single mechanical unit. (See Figures 6.12 and 6.13.)

Take Your Stance. A balanced setup is used, as in traditional strokes, but in this stroke, placing slightly more weight on the left foot would be beneficial, although not required. The shoulders, due to the left

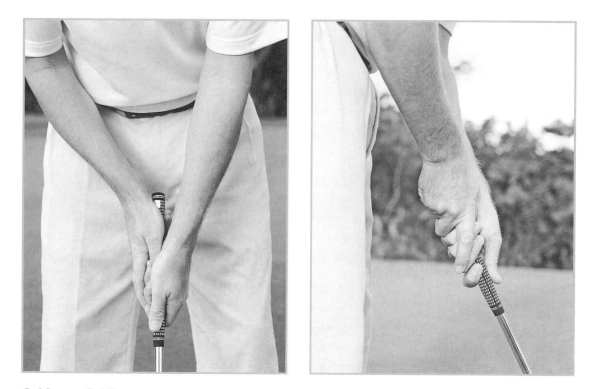

6.12 and **6.13.** The left hand in this stroke is positioned lower than the right hand. Notice the right forefinger extended over the fingers of the left hand to create more stability.

hand being lower, will be positioned more level to the ground. The forward shoulder may even be a slight bit lower. (See Figure 6.14.) Level is the desired outcome. The ball position needs to be forward of the middle of the stance and at the bottom of the stroke. Because this stroke places the hands in a position that is ahead of the ball, it creates a steeper angle of attack, and the bottom of the stroke will be altered from a traditional location to a little more forward in the stance. You will need to experiment a little to locate the exact position where your putter bottoms out. A good estimation would put the ball about two ball widths forward of center.

Stroke the Putt. The mechanics of this stroke will be exactly the same as the two traditional strokes. Because the shoulders in this

6.14. You can use either a straight-back straight-through or inside-square-inside swing path with this stroke. This example is following an inside-square-inside path. The shoulders are controlling the stroke.

stroke are more level to the ground, as opposed to the traditional tilt of the other strokes, I find this stroke creates better success with a straight-back straight-through path. The shoulders' positioning combined with the rocking motion will keep the putter head closer to the ground throughout the stroke. This results in creating a shallow angle of attack and puts a very smooth roll on the ball.

Claw Stroke

This stroke found its way onto the PGA Tour in a most unique fashion. A Wisconsin local at Brown Deer Golf Course taught this stroke to a teenage boy who played at the club. The boy grew up and became a very fine player, in spite of not using the stroke. The boy happened to be Skip Kendall, a PGA Tour pro who during a rain delay in an event in Florida happened to recall the stroke and passed the knowledge on to a fellow player who was about to lose his tour card. That player was Chris Dimarco, and at the time he was putting himself off the tour so he gave the stroke a try. By changing to the claw stroke, Dimarco putted his way not only to a steady position on the tour but also to several victories. He has since become one of the steadiest competitors on the PGA Tour. The main advantage to this putting style is that by positioning the lower hand in a claw fashion, the player can make a smoother, more natural stroke. The lower hand grip is similar to the grip that a violinist would use. This position takes excessive wrist action out of the stroke. Since the time Dimarco started using the claw stroke, several other players have either used it as well or used a version similar to it. Some of the other players who have competed with this stroke are Tom Kite,

Mark O'Meara, Jeff Sluman, Billy Andrade, Tim Clark, Andy Bean, and Mark Calcavechia.

The Stroke's Theory. This stroke is also used for curing problems with the previous traditional strokes. Positioning the right hand in this unique manner changes the feel and mechanics of the putt. This type of stroke is not one a beginner would use. It would instead be used by a player who is struggling with controlling the putter face throughout a putt. This unique grip is actually a more natural position for the human hand. (See Figure 6.15.) Think about how you hold a pencil. This is the grip mechanics that this stroke is trying to apply. It is an easier, less manipulated way for the dominant hand to hold the putter. Any putter that you would use for a traditional straight-back straight-through stroke would be just as effective for this stroke.

6.15. The arm positions are what make this stroke. See how the right arm is in a pistonlike position and the left forearm is perfectly in line with the shaft.

Grip the Putter. The only different mechanic for this stroke from a traditional stroke is the grip. The grip for the claw stroke consists of the left hand in a traditional top position but the right hand turned upside down, with the palm facing toward the body. Because of the grip, the hand's position at setup is centered between the hips, without any forward press. The right arm will be bent. The forearm will be positioned almost parallel to the intended line. This, combined with a bent posture, will help eliminate unwanted wrist movement and a straight-back straight-through path. (See Figures 6.16 and 6.17.)

Take Your Stance. As this stroke uses a straight-back straight-through path, you will want to use the very same positions as those found in the traditional straight-back straight-through stroke. The only difference is that the grip is changed to the new claw position of the right hand. This position will cause the right elbow to be forced

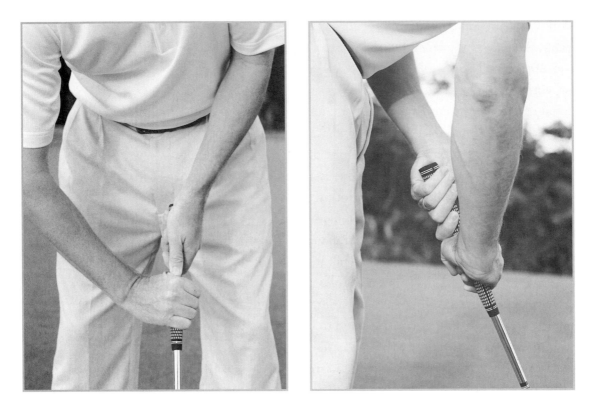

6.16 and **6.17.** The lower hand position puts the right forearm parallel to the target line.

away from the body. This will position the right forearm to a more parallel position with the intended line. Exactly parallel would be ideal, but some players will feel too much tension in the hands and arm. To alleviate the tension, a position just less than parallel would be acceptable.

Stroke the Putt.   Again, the stroke will be nearly identical to the straight-back straight-through stroke. The claw grip of the right hand is the key change. When making the stroke, the right arm—because of its position away from the body—is in a great position to act like a piston. Stroke the putt by making sure to keep the right elbow as close to parallel to the intended line as possible. This will ensure the best success for a straight-back straight-through path.

Belly Putter Stroke

The true creator of the belly putter stroke is unknown. There is a story of the stroke being created by Paul Runyan and Phil Rodgers a few decades ago. Mr. Runyan was a good putter and player and had a great career as a teaching professional. He created a split-hand grip that he used and had a longer putter to accommodate the taller stance. As the story goes, one day Mr. Rodgers decided to stick it into his belly and use it that way. There is a second story, and this one gets the stroke in the hands of a tour champion. Scotty Cameron, the great putter designer, explained his theory: "We put lasers upside down [in the grip] in a putter, and that laser should point at the belly button throughout the stroke." Paul Azinger proceeded to ask the question that, if the butt of the putter was supposed to point at the belly button throughout the stroke: "Why don't I just stick it in my belly button?" Mr. Azinger went on to win the 2001 Hawaiian Open with the belly putter stroke, which has led to many other great players using it, including Vijay Singh, Stewart Cink, Lee Westwood, Billy Mayfair, Ian Woosnam, Fred Couples, Gary Accord, Colin Montgomerie, Stacy Prammana-sudh, Trevor Immelman, Sergio Garcia, and Mark Calcavechia.

The Stroke's Theory.   This stroke is a modification to the traditional stroke. To create better control of the putter head and create a proper pendulum motion, a pivot point is necessary. In the traditional stroke, the putter is not anchored to create a solid pivot point. The pivot point in the traditional stroke is found within the body, at the base of the neck and collarbone. By extending the length of a traditional putter and using traditional mechanics, the putter will solidly anchor to the body at the belly button. This creates a very solid single pivot point. The putter can be of a traditional design, although it will need

6.18. The butt end of the grip is anchored just above the belly button.

to be longer. Depending on your fit, the mid-length putter can be anywhere from thirty-six to forty-five inches in length.

Grip the Putter. Any type of grip can work with this stroke. The main difference with this stroke is that the hands grip the putter down the shaft from the butt of the putter. This leaves enough putter length to be positioned into or up to two inches above the belly button. For this stroke to be effective, the butt of the putter needs to be firmly touching the belly and remain there throughout the motion. (See Figure 6.18.) The arms should be relaxed with a slight bend at the elbows, which will be pointing at the hips. The arms will make a classic Y position with the putter shaft, which helps keep the stroke very solid.

Take Your Stance. Place your feet square to the intended line, and have your hips and shoulders follow suit. The position of the eyes will be inside the ball position for an inside-square-inside path and over the ball for straight-back straight-through. Your body type will dictate your posture. The lower to the ground the belly is, the more erect the posture. The higher off the ground, the more bent the posture. Whatever the posture is at setup, it will need to remain the same throughout the stroke.

Stroke the Putt. Making a proper belly putter stroke requires that you maintain the pivot point that has been created by placing the butt of the putter into the belly. (See Figure 6.19.) To maintain this point through the stroke, you will need to keep the belly steady. To keep the belly steady, you must also keep the hips steady. You will need to focus on making a nice smooth and slow stroke while keeping the upper body still. Any upper-body motion can cause the hips to move, which will cause the belly to move, which causes a missed putt. To create a straight-back straight-through swing path, you will need to focus on moving the putter by only moving the arms and hands. If you want to create an arcing swing path, you will need to allow the upper body to turn along with the putter head so the body and putter head follow the proper arc. This is the more difficult path to master with this stroke, due to the fact that the upper-body motion may cause the hips to turn, causing the belly to turn, causing the pivot point to be lost.

Stand-Up Stroke

Charlie Owens created this stroke in 1985. The putter he used for this stroke was nicknamed Slim Jim and was forty-six inches long. In the first years this stroke was played, the United States Golf Association (USGA), the rules governing body for golf in America, had very healthy discussions as to the legality of its use. The USGA finally decided that the stroke was legal. The first player to win a PGA tournament with this stroke was Rocco Mediate. He had terrible back problems and found that he could putt well with a long putter. He won the 1991 Doral-Ryder Open. A longer putter allows the player to stand erect and use a sweeping motion when making the putting stroke. When a player has a more erect stance, there is less stress on the back, excess body and wrist motion is eliminated, and the putter can be anchored to the body. This anchoring creates a single pivot point in the motion of the stroke. A single pivot point makes the putting motion more of a fine motor skill activity, like writing or painting. The stand-up stroke is used by at least 10 percent of the play-

6.19. This is a setup for an inside-square-inside swing path. The putter remains anchored to the belly throughout the stroke.

ers on the Senior Tour and has been a favorite of a good number of other professionals, including Tim Clark, Beth Daniel, Nick O'Hern, Sam Torrence, Shingo Katayama, Rocco Mediate, Sandy Lyle, Scott McCarron, Colin Montgomerie, Lanny Watkins, Tom Lehman, Bernhard Langer, and Mike Hulbert.

The Stroke's Theory.   The idea behind this stroke is that when a player stands more erect, stress on the back can be reduced or eliminated. By splitting the hands, more control is put into the dominant hand and arm. By anchoring the butt end of the putter against the sternum, a secure pivot point is created, from which an ideal pendulum motion can be created. The putter to use for this stroke is nontraditional. It needs to be long. The proper length will depend on your stature, but regardless, the top of the putter at your address position needs to be about the height of a logo positioned on your golf shirt. The lie angle needs to be adjusted to fit the more upright position.

Grip the Putter.   The grip for this stroke is very important. The left hand anchors the butt of the top of the putter grip against the sternum by placing the thumb on top of the grip with the remaining fingers lightly wrapped around the grip. The right hand can be held in many different ways. (See Figures 6.20 and 6.21.) It can be held like that of a traditional grip with the thumb on top of the grip, the palm facing the target, and the rest of the fingers wrapped around the grip. It can also be gripped in a more natural way, like you would grip a pencil. Hold the grip between your forefinger and thumb, with the forefinger on top of the grip and the thumb under. The rest of the fingers curl into the palm. Whichever way you choose to grip, the right hand will be fine as long as it allows you to keep the putter's face square at impact. The right arm will need to be slightly bent, and the amount of bend will depend on the posture.

Take Your Stance.   The stance is positioned square to the intended line of putt, with the hips and shoulders square as well. The posture is the unique feature of this stroke. Instead of the traditional bend at

6.20 and **6.21.** The top hand securely holds the butt of the grip against the sternum.

the waist, you stand more erect with only a slight bend at the waist. You only need enough bend to allow the putter to swing clear of your body. To create a straight-back straight-through path, your posture will need to bend enough to allow the putter shaft to be nearly vertical, while keeping the eyes directly over the ball. To create an arcing path, stand more erect and allow the shaft to be at an angle. This will correctly put the eyes inside the ball position. The ball position will be generally in the center of the stance. Find where the putter swings level to the ground, and place the ball according to that position.

Stroke the Putt.   There are two methods to produce this stroke. You can use the common mechanics of rocking the shoulders, or you can eliminate shoulder motion by bending and straightening the right arm. In this method, the right arm pulls the putter on the back stroke and then pushes it on the through stroke. You want to maintain a steady upper body so your chest and left hand can act as a secure anchor for the pendulum stroke. In the rocking method, the right arm will remain steady, and the shoulders create the pendulum motion and are the only moving power source. (See Figure 6.22.)

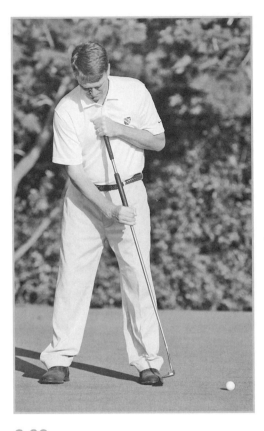

6.22. This setup is positioned for a straight-back straight-through path, by having a little bend in the posture and by having the eyes directly over the ball.

Sidesaddle Stroke

As previously mentioned, this stroke was first made popular by Sam Snead in the late 1960s. Most of the players using this type of stroke today use a longer putter. Mr. Snead's original sidesaddle has undergone several different name modifications, due to the fact that some players use a different length putter. Some other names that I have heard used for this stroke are the face-on stroke and the face-forward stroke. Both are similar to the sidesaddle in that they have the body and eyes facing the target with the ball positioned to the side. The modern modifications make the stroke even easier as they anchor the top of the long putter to the body to create a single joint motion. The only professionals I can recall who have dared to play with this easy stroke besides Snead are Grant Waite, Bob Jensen, and Peter Lonard.

The Stroke's Theory. Sam Snead felt this stroke was like throwing horseshoes. Others say this stroke is as simple as throwing a ball underhand. These concepts create the theory behind the stroke. Find a simple motion that even a child can perform, and apply it to putting. By facing the target, positioning the ball directly under the shoulder, and swinging forward with the dominant arm (not across the body like traditional strokes), you can achieve a simple and effective method of putting the ball the desired direction with distance control. If you have never tried this stroke before, do the following exercise to see just how easy it can be. Take three golf balls and stand on the green about fifteen feet from a hole. Toss the balls toward the hole. Look to see how you stood and tossed the balls. I bet you stood facing the hole and tossed the balls underhand.

The putter to use for this stroke is unique. It needs to be long and as upright a lie as the rules will allow. It also needs to have a long or split grip to allow for the separation of the hands. There are many makers of this type of putter, and most of the major putter manufacturers have a long putter model.

Grip the Putter. The left hand anchors the butt of the top of the putter grip by placing the thumb on top of the club and wrapping the remaining fingers around the grip lightly. The hand and top of the grip are then placed against the shoulder joint to create an anchored position. The left forearm is positioned to rest gently across the chest. The right hand is positioned onto the lower grip, which is anywhere from one to two feet below the top of the grip, creating a 90-degree angle at the elbow joint, in one of two manners: like Sam Snead held the club, with the palm of the right hand facing the hole, the thumb held down the side of the grip, and the remaining fingers closing around the grip; or in a more natural position of the hand, by having the grip rest between the thumb and forefingers, similar to the claw grip.

Take Your Stance. You can place your feet in any comfortable manner, but the most efficient way is to point both toes in the general direction of your starting line. More specifically, make sure the right foot is parallel to the line you intend the ball to begin on. You will have more weight (approximately 80 percent) on your right foot than your left. I recommend keeping the feet closer together and no

6.23. This unique stance has the body facing the hole, more like how you would toss a ball underhand, instead of the traditional stance of square to the intended line.

more than eight inches apart. With the feet in place, make sure the shoulders are positioned perpendicular, or 90 degrees, to your target line. They need to be square to your target line for success. You can determine your perfect ball position by experimenting with finding the bottom of your stroke where the putter is moving level to the ground. This will be different for everyone, but a general rule is the ball position is about five inches outside the right toe and anywhere from just behind the toe to six inches out in front (most commonly equal to the toe). Because putter head sizes vary, think about never letting the heel of the putter be farther from your foot than a couple of inches. The head should be positioned in a manner that allows the eyes to remain parallel to the ground, with the right eye directly over the line of the putt. Ideally, the eyes will be looking at the hole during the stroke. Just like a baseball player throwing a ball or a basketball player shooting a hoop, you look at your target. (See Figure

INSIDE-SQUARE-INSIDE STROKE

This stroke uses the traditional square-to-the-intended-line setup positions. Because this stroke resembles the rest of your golf shots, there is not a lot of modification from hitting the woods and irons. So as long as your golf swing is good, you can create a good putting stroke.

The hands, wrists, elbows, and shoulders all stay connected and work as a single unit rotating around the body to create a naturally arcing stroke.

This stroke, when used by an adept player, provides great feel. You can use this feel to create a great putting touch on the greens.

STRAIGHT-BACK STRAIGHT-THROUGH STROKE

A proper setup with feet, knees, hips, and shoulders all parallel to the intended line will allow this stroke to perform at its best.

With practice and a good set of mechanics, this stroke will keep the putter's head always on the intended line of putt, with the putter's face always perfectly square to that intended line.

You can take this stroke with confidence onto any speed of green. The faster the green speed, the better this stroke performs.

CLAW STROKE

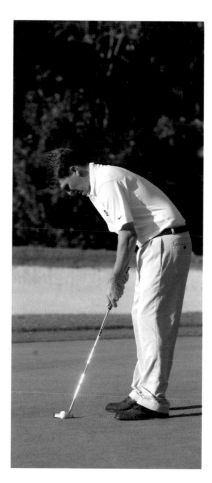  

When you position the hands opposite of traditional, with the left hand below the right, you create the ability to eliminate any unwanted wrist action from the stroke.

This stroke uses either set of a traditional stroke's mechanics. You can use either the straight-back straight-through swing path or the inside-square-inside swing path. The modified grip of this stroke can fix problems found within the other traditional strokes.

If you have problems controlling distance or have the yips caused by the hands and wrists, this stroke is an excellent option.

CROSS-HANDED STROKE

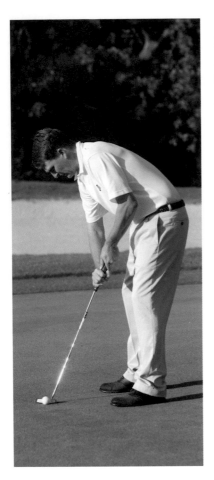  

If you are having problems with your straight-back straight-through traditional stroke, like pulls or pushes, the grip of this stroke in its unique position can help to solve those problems.

With the right hand positioned in a manner that is more reminiscent of holding a pencil, this stroke becomes less controlled by the wrists and more controlled by the arms and shoulders.

If you want to improve your control over a straight-back straight-through swing path and your problem is overactive wrist action, then this stroke might be the best option for you.

BELLY PUTTER STROKE

This stroke requires the use of a midlength putter. The putter needs to be long enough to be positioned into the belly button area when you are in a traditional square-to-the-intended-line setup position.

With the putter anchored into the body, you can use a single power source of shoulders to create a perfect pendulum motion.

Anyone who has trouble keeping his or her traditional inside-square-inside stroke steady would gain an instant advantage by securing the end of the putter to the belly. As long as the lower body remains steady, there is no need to worry about the swing path being incorrect.

STAND-UP STROKE

If you want to make sure you hole out the short putts more often, then you want to use a perfect pendulum motion. By standing more upright and using a long putter that can be secured to the body, you can create that desired pendulum motion.

The left hand's only job is to secure the butt of the grip to the body and keep it there throughout the stroke. This makes sure that the only hand making the motion is the more dominant right hand.

Not only do players with bad backs find this stroke to be exceptional, but players who are jittery with their current traditional stroke due to unwanted wrist motion find that making the change to a long putter instantly improves their putting average.

SIDESADDLE STROKE

This stroke places the body and eyes toward the hole instead of the traditional facing-the-target line. This has unique advantages. There is no concern for a dominant eye because the eyes will remain level, and it eliminates the desire to move the body and peek.

The setup positions place the club securely against the body to create a pivot point. The right arm becomes the power source, which can be swung like you would move your arm to toss a ball. This makes this stroke the easiest of all putting strokes.

If you are totally results-oriented and can get over how unorthodox this stroke looks, you will easily become a better putter using it.

SPLIT-HAND STROKE

The hands are separated to give you a distinct advantage. When the hands are spread, there can be no unwanted wrist action, and the manner in which the hands are placed puts the dominant hand in control of the motion and stroke.

The stance is open at a 45-degree angle, which gives you an advantage with the eyes being level and facing the target and placing the body in a more naturally athletic position, thus eliminating a lot of problems that the traditional strokes carry.

If you have grown up playing other athletic games, then using this stroke will be the most natural fit for you. When you use a stroke that is a natural fit, there are fewer mechanics that you need to be concerned with, and it's always better to have fewer mechanics to worry about.

6.23.) If you cannot get used to looking at your target, it is acceptable to look at the ball. The feet, hips, and shoulders are positioned to face the target, and all should be in line with each other. The tendency in this stroke is to allow the shoulders to rotate toward the ball, because the ball is placed to the side of the body. Make sure the shoulders remain perpendicular to the target line. The posture in this stroke should be a slight bend forward, but closer to fully erect than bent over, unless you use a traditional-length putter the Sam Snead way. Your posture will fit to the length of the putter.

Stroke the Putt. The stroke is more like tossing a ball underhand than a traditional golf stroke. With the left hand acting as an anchor and the right hand positioned under the shoulder, the motion will allow the shoulder to move freely to create a perfect pendulum stroke. The putter is moved straight back and straight through the target line using only the dominant right hand and arm. (See Figure 6.24.) The left hand and wrist only have a slight rotation, which allows the putter to move smoothly. If you are gripping the Sam Snead way, the right forearm should actually touch the shaft and remain there for the entire stroke to help stabilize the putter head for maximum control.

6.24. See how the ball is positioned to the side while the body remains facing the hole. The dominant right hand and arm create and control the motion.

Split-Hand Stroke

This stroke was created by Jim Alvarez, a former hockey player who, due to a hamstring injury, had his golfing restricted to the practice putting green. He had to find an easier way to putt with the injury. He discovered that if he just stood more upright and turned toward the hole, he could putt even with the injured hamstring. A side effect of this setup was that he found it easier to make putts. He knew he had a stroke that was effective for him. In trying to master his stroke, he realized he needed to create a putter to properly accommodate this unique style, as there were none on the market. Alvarez created the putter and the split-hand stroke in 1999 and has been bringing the idea to the world ever since. The stroke can be best described as looking like a hockey slap shot. The stance is open at about a 45-degree angle, which allows both eyes to directly face the hole. The hands grip the club in a split manner, which allows for good dominant arm control. The stroke also allows you to stand straighter and puts you in a single plane, so you can take the putter straight back and straight through down your target line. With only a few tour-level players using this stroke, it might be a little while before we see it used in a victory on the PGA Tour. I do believe though that it is only a matter of time before this stroke proves its real value to the game of putting. It is currently being used by LPGA player Natalie Gulbis. Other touring professionals who have used this stroke include Leslie Spalding, Michelle Estill, Greg Smith, and Doug Sanders.

The Stroke's Theory. The theory behind this stroke is that to make putting more effective, a putting stroke should be used that allows for a more natural and athletic setup and motion. Anyone who has shot a hockey puck or bunted a baseball knows that the most effective method is to turn the body more toward the target, split the hands from each other, and push the stick or bat into and through the puck or ball toward the target. This split-hand stroke accomplishes the fundamentals and ease of a bunt. This stroke is actually easier than a bunt. This is because a golf ball is not flying ninety miles an hour at you; it is just sitting there waiting to be hit. Due to the mechanics involved, it is a great stroke for creating a straight-back straight-through path. To make this stroke work, you are going to need a custom putter. The putter is a split-grip, midlength putter with a flatter than normal lie

6.25 and **6.26.** The hands are separated with the thumbs aligned on the top of the shaft.

angle. Alvarez named the putter that he created for this stroke the hammY, because of his original hamstring injury.

Grip the Putter.   One of the unique features of this stroke is the grip. The two hands are separated from each other and for good reason. (See Figures 6.25 and 6.26.) Think about baseball for a moment. In trying to hit a home run, the player will hold the bat with the hands close to each other. This helps create leverage and power. Now if this player was called to bunt, what is the first thing the player does? The player spreads his or her hands for control. In putting we are looking for more control than distance, so in this stroke, we spread the hands.

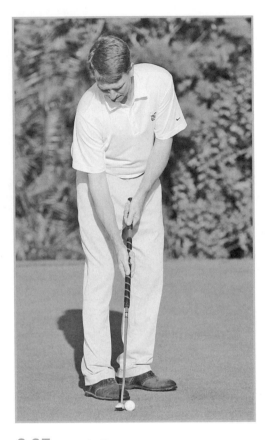

6.27. The ball position is played opposite the rear toe, with the dominant eye over the ball.

The left hand is positioned on the putter just as if you were to shake someone's hand—thumb on the top, with the rest of the fingers wrapped around the club. This hand simply works as a guide. The left arm is positioned snugly against the left side. It will remain there throughout the stroke. The right hand is positioned on the club on the lower grip of the putter, about two feet below the left-hand position. The arm should be mostly but not completely extended. A slight bend is good for helping to maintain a good feel. The right hand needs to have the palm facing the target.

Take Your Stance. This is the second unique feature of this stroke. The stance is one that is considered in golf terms to be open. The feet and hips should be open roughly 45 degrees from the target line. I say roughly because variation from this is acceptable. The main purpose of the open stance is to allow you to see the line, take the left side out of play, and put your right arm in control of the putt. As long as you remain comfortable and open, then the stance is correct. The shoulders will be slightly less open than the hips and feet but will definitely be open to the target line. The ball is positioned back in your stance, opposite your right toe. (See Figure 6.27.) Because the putter will be extended away from the body, the ball will need to be placed away from the body and in front of the putter. Everyone is different, so you will need to experiment to determine the exact distance that works for you. The head and eyes will be turned toward the target at almost a 45-degree angle to your target line. If you can place your head and eyes directly over the ball, you will be better able to see your intended line and help to create a straight-back straight-through stroke. When you strike the putt, you will be looking at the ball. If you practice this stroke while looking at the hole, you will help to create the trust of the stroke and learn to allow the right arm to do the stroking.

Stroke the Putt. Once you have comfortable setup positions and have made sure the putter face is square to the intended line, you are ready to stroke the putt. Throughout the stroke, keep the left arm snug against the left side. The left arm makes no motion in this stroke. With the right arm, move the hand and putter's face straight back down the target line, and swing forward through the ball straight down the target line. (See Figure 6.28.) This will create a straight-back straight-through path. The feel of the stroke should resemble the feel of tossing a ball to a target. The follow-through will have the putter face square to the intended line, and the putter will remain on the straight-back straight-through path.

6.28. The hands are split. The left forearm is in line with the shaft. The elbow is tucked into the side. The dominant right arm makes the stroke. See how the right palm remains square to the target line.

CHOOSE YOUR STYLE

Now that you have seen that there are eight successful types of putting strokes that have been used by tournament professionals, you need to find the one that works best for your game. If you observe the tours closely, you will see many different players trying different strokes and different putters. When you were reading the names of the players using the different strokes, you undoubtedly saw that some of the players were listed under more than one stroke. This is because even the great players will try a new stroke if it has promise of improving their putting averages. These players, like you, are searching for the stroke that will make them more putts. Thoughtful experimentation is the method that most use to find the right stroke.

The thoughtful part is knowing the strengths and weaknesses of your putting stroke. For instance, if your strengths include good alignment and an accurate straight-back straight-through path, but your weakness is unwanted wrist action, then a great stroke to experiment with would be either the claw grip stroke or the cross-handed stroke.

The experimentation part is needed because the only way to know if a stroke is going to give success is by playing and practicing with it. Anytime you experiment with a new style, you will want to learn the unique mechanics in your home. Once you have the basic mechanics, take it to a practice green and go through a good practice routine. Practice a few times before you take it to the course for a trial. After just a few trials on the course, you will likely have an idea as to whether or not the style will work for you. If it does not, then you can experiment with a different one. Eventually, you will find one that works best. Use the color images in the insert to help you decide which will be your best fit.

chapter

7

CHOOSING A PUTTER

When you play with a custom-fit putter, your chances of holing putts increase dramatically. The old golf adage "It is the Indian, not the arrow, that makes a bad shot" only holds true if the Indian has a perfectly straight and balanced arrow. In golf, a great golfer can make a putt with any putter and any old ball. But will that golfer be as consistently proficient at making putts over the long haul of eighteen holes? Not a chance. The arrow is definitely the reason in this case. The proper putter can make you a better player simply because you know that the putter is doing its job correctly and that there is absolutely no chance a missed putt was caused by faulty equipment. If you are confident that the putting tool was not at fault (even though it does make a great excuse), you can more clearly focus on the true cause of the miss, which must be either the reading of the green or a skills or mechanics problem. You can then fix the cause of the miss before the next putt. In other words, it must be the Indian, not the arrow.

Even though you can use any club to make a putt, the putter itself is specifically designed to do the job most effectively. Original putters were created to help the golfers move the balls on what were then bumpy and most challenging putting surfaces. The greens of years prior are not what golfers play on today. The grass types were native grasses and were generally mown by flocks of sheep, if mown at all. The original putter designs were made to be most effective on those types of conditions. As time has progressed, the grass varieties have improved, and the maintenance methods have improved to make the grass as smooth as silk in some instances. To accommodate these new conditions, putter design has been modified.

Modern putters come in an endless number of designs and variations. They are all designed to basically accomplish the same goal, to get the ball rolling smoothly toward the hole. The proper putter will get the ball rolling on top of the blades of grass quickly after contact, will start the ball rolling in the correct direction, will allow for proper gauging of distance, and will allow you to aim correctly. An improper putter can cause the ball to go in the wrong direction, can interfere with your ability to gauge distance by causing an inconsistent roll, and will not allow the ball to roll smoothly after contact.

Q&A WITH BOBBY GRACE

To find out just how important the putter is to the game of golf, I interviewed one of golf's greatest putter designers, Bobby Grace. (See Figure 7.1.)

Brian Lake: How long have you been designing putters?

Bobby Grace: Since 1991.

BL: Why do you enjoy designing putters?

BG: When I wanted to make a career out of designing golf equipment, I was advised by a well-respected golf pro to focus on the tools that the players feel would make them the most money: the driver, wedges, and putter. Metalwoods were coming out, and there were classic wedges on the scene, so I focused on the putter. It is the only club

7.1. Putter designer Bobby Grace shows off some of the custom putters he has designed for players on the PGA Tour.

in the bag known as the total equalizer. If your opponent can outdrive you with a long drive but cannot make an eight-footer, and you make every eight-footer you look at, you will win most every time.

BL: Would you agree with the old statement "It is the Indian, not the arrow" when it comes to putting?

BG: No way. The Indian is important. If you don't have technique, then it doesn't matter what putter you use. But without a proper putter, good technique becomes stifled. Put a broom handle in Tiger Woods's hands, and I will beat him. There are the great putters who probably could putt with anything and still be great because they have a great ability for natural compensation. These special players are few. Most players cannot compensate well enough to overcome a poor putter.

Besides, most players learn their feel for putting with the putter that they have used over the years. Take that particular putter away from them and let them play with something different and their putting will falter. The arrow is very important. I feel that there has to be a blend between technique and a properly fit putter.

BL: Can a player become a great putter without a properly fit putter?

BG: A player can be a good putter without a fit putter, but the player could be even better with a properly fit putter.

BL: Are there any tools other than the putter that you would consider important to great putting?

BG: A laser-alignment tool. Most players do not realize how off their aiming alignment actually is. This is a great tool for fitting a person to a putter head and its alignment method. Putters have aiming lines and such in many different patterns. This tool allows you to find which alignment method and putter head work best for you.

BL: How much focus do you impart when designing a putter, in regard to playing conditions (grass types and speed), players' putting styles (traditional, belly, stand-up, and so on), and stroke methods (straight-back straight-through or inside-square-inside swing paths)?

BG: Not so much for grass types, but quite a lot for styles and stroke methods. I design mostly for the tour players, and I have to be ready for everyone. With the design capabilities of the putters I make, I can offer over a hundred fitting combinations to precisely fit the player. I have a new design with a switchable faceplate, which offers custom options. We introduced changeable weights to the market, which offers great design capabilities. We even have a putter head that is designed to accommodate both a square-to-square stroke and an arcing path by simply changing the shaft. Because good players use different types of strokes, I have to have all of the putter style options for those players, so we offer a full line of different types of putters.

BL: If you were to custom-build a putter for someone who would like to become a great putter, what personal information would you require from the player, and what putter design variables would you need to customize for that particular player?

BG: I need to see a player—how they stroke a putt, what type of putter they use. And I need to learn how they already make a putting stroke. If the player has a problem that is fixable, we fix the problem and then fit for a putter. If the problem was not going to be fixed, then I would fit the putter around the problem.

BL: Do you agree with the USGA rules of golf that define the design parameters of putters?

BG: Yes. There are a couple I don't care for, but yes. I have a good standing with the USGA in that I have not had a putter design that they have not allowed to be played in a tournament. Even with new designs that I submit to the USGA, what takes normally fourteen weeks to get approved I usually get approved in a couple of days. I design my putters within the USGA parameters. I push the edge but within the rules.

BL: If you ignored the USGA rules, could you create a putter that would make the skills of golf unimportant?

BG: No. There is no way to take the skills out of play from putting. A tiny bit, yes I could peck away at eliminating some of the skills.

BL: How would you help a player choose a style of putter to use (mallet, blade, modified blade, nontraditional, and so on)?

BG: This is a question I get asked quite a bit. I deal with the tour players. They mostly choose based on what is pleasing to their eye. I have some trouble trying to convince a player to try a new look of a putter, even though the putter is much better performing. I try to convince them to not look at the putter but to just go by how the ball reacts. Some players give the new styles a try; others are stuck on traditional looks.

BL: Putter heads can be made from so many different types of materials. What is your favorite material for putters, and why?

BG: Aluminum for the frames, tungsten for the weight. Aluminum is light, so I can build larger putter heads, and then I use tungsten as the material to give the proper weight to the putter. In years prior, players would use lead tape to add weight to the putter. I can professionally alter weight by using tungsten or copper-tungsten inserts without the messy look of lead tape.

BL: Does it matter much at all as to the size and type of grip you use on your putter?

BG: Yes. The grip is huge. From a 1962 Wilson catalog, there is a quote for the putter that is regarded as one of the best putters ever produced, and it says, "Especially designed by Arnold Palmer. Perfect head feel transmitted to the grip." A good grip will set properly in the hands and will allow you to have great feel and a sense of what is going on when you strike a putt. Larger size grips can even take the wrists out of the stroke. Take a player used to a particular type of grip and change it on him, and you will see just how important the grip is. He is going to struggle with the different grip.

BL: How important is the length of a putter?

BG: This is one thing that most people have wrong. The wrong length of putter will create bad posture and other bad habits. You can adjust to a wrong shaft, like gripping down, but you are adjusting. If you practice long and hard enough, you might even get good with the adjustment. Who wants to waste their time trying to bandage their stroke with compensations that may or may not work? It is pretty important to have the correct length.

BL: As players—children or adults—develop their putting game, how often do you think they should reevaluate the putter they are using?

BG: I personally have taught my children the belly putter stroke. It is a stroke that does not allow for breakdown and keeps the arms in great positions. I also have taught them a traditional stroke. This is because the USGA can change rules, and I wouldn't want my children to know only the belly putter stroke and then have that stroke banned.

BL: Are you saying that if you were not worried about the rules changing, your children would only putt belly putter style?

BG: Yes.

BL: As I understand that you have a large collection of the world's best putters ever made, and you possess the skills and knowledge to create some of the world's best putters, how do you choose what putter you are going to play with when you really want to putt well?

BG: I played eleven years around the world with the Palmer 8852 and made a lot of putts with that putter. I had to actually sell it to make myself play with my putters. If I were going to play on superfast undulating greens, though, I would play with the best putter I have ever made. I made a putter similar to, and better than, the Palmer 8852, which was played by Jose Maria Olazabal. He went on to place second at the 2006 Masters and shot a final-round 66 with it. He recently returned the putter to me. It is very rare for a player to return a putter. Most players who have had success with a putter keep hold of it.

BL: How important is putting to the game of golf?

BG: There is a famous quote from legendary Willie Parks. "The person who can putt is a match for everyone." I think that says it all.

If Bobby Grace feels that strongly about the importance of putting and a putter—and more importantly, about a properly fit putter—I highly recommend finding the proper putter fit to you.

HOW TO CHOOSE THE PROPER PUTTER FOR YOU

Some players, without even knowing it, use a nonscientific approach to fitting themselves for a putter. They keep hitting different putters until they finally find one that works. Finding the proper putter just for you can be a challenge, but you do not have to buy a hundred putters to find it. There is an ideal putter for every player, and finding the right putter is easy if you follow the proper procedures. When choosing your putter, you need to be aware of the following issues:

- ► The putter must be legal according to the rules of golf that you play.
- ► The putter must fit you and your individual putting stroke.
- ► You must be comfortable with the look and feel of the putter.
- ► The cost of the putter must be within your budget. (Though if the piece you need is too expensive, you might need to consider mortgaging the house or selling off one of your extra organs so you can make it work for your budget—a good putter is that important!)

There are only two valid reasons to get a new putter. First is because you need one that properly fits you and your stroke, and second, because you have "misplaced" your putter up in a tree. The objective in choosing a putter is to find the correct combination of variables that best fit you and your putting stroke. Examine the following fitting variables to assist you in making the best putter choice.

Rules

Appendix II of the *United States Golf Association Rules of Golf* book is ten pages long and covers the design limitations put on putters. By understanding a few rules that affect putter design, you will be better off in making decisions regarding some of the remaining variables. The overall length of a putter must be at least eighteen inches with no limit above that. That is why long putters are permitted. There are specific alignment requirements that are measured when the putter is in its normal address position. Unless you are designing your own putter, there is no need to go into great detail about this. The shaft has requirements as well, and again, this is not important unless you are a putter designer. There are club head requirements, including the club's face, which are also geared toward designers. The grip is an important equipment detail that you can make decisions on, because the rules allow for variations. The reason the putter grip can be different from regular grips is that a putter grip may have a noncircular cross section (flat edge). The rules give you insight into some of the restrictions the USGA places on the design of putters.

Style

There are as many styles of putter heads as there are greens to putt on, but I have made it manageable by breaking them down into five variations:

- ► Mallet
- ► Blade
- ► Modified blade
- ► Untraditional
- ► Illegal (according to the USGA rules)

The putter head style selection is more about it looking good to you than the performance concerns. Some putter head styles, however, have been designed with only performance in mind. They have weight and balance features, as well as aiming and alignment features, which will enhance the performance of the putter. When selecting a putter head style, the first thing to look for is whether it looks good to your eye when you hold it next to a ball. This really isn't very scientific; the style is more about confidence than anything else. When you place the putter behind a ball, do you feel confident that it is capable of making a putt?

There is some function behind the aesthetic that you want to be aware of when choosing a putter head. When you look at the different

7.2. Putters come in four basic legal head styles and three common lengths. You can put any head style on any of the three lengths.

styles, notice that the differences are in the lines and curves of the material. These lines and curves serve to assist you with aiming a putt. Some people aim better using perpendicular lines, others are better using horizontal lines, while yet others are better using curves or circles. You will have to decide which fits your eye through trial and error. (See Figure 7.2.)

Brand

Once you have chosen a style of putter, you will need to find a company that makes what you need. Choosing a company and brand is a personal decision. Most of the companies that sell putters have a selection of each of the styles. I recommend for putters that you go with the age-old adage "You get what you pay for." Study the market and choose a company and brand that will not erode your confidence. Just because a cheap putter may look exactly the same as a high-end putter does not mean that the quality in materials is the same. What you lose in a cheaper product, besides quality control, is the feel and feedback of superior materials.

Length

The length of the putter needs to be proper for your height at your putting address position and for the particular stroke that you play with. The length could change over time as you improve or change your mechanics and skills, have changes in your body type, or have physical problems that require specific modification. Checking your putter's length is something you will want to do every once in a while. I will explain how to choose the proper length of putter for each of the strokes so you can be fit for length with whichever stroke you use.

▶ **Traditional length.** Assume your normal putting address position without the putter in hand. Someone should assist you by placing the putter head on the ground, directly beneath your eyes, and the putter grip into your hands, being careful not to move your hands to find the grip. You will want one inch of grip above your top hand for the perfect length putter. Have your assistant mark the putter at the one-inch mark. Now measure from the mark, down the putter shaft to the bottom of the putter head. This measurement will be the proper putter length for you. I recommend doing this procedure several times to correct for any inconsistency in your setup. The more times you do it, the better chance you have of determining an accurate average that is your perfect putter length. Traditional-length putters range anywhere from eighteen to thirty-six inches.

▶ **Belly putter length.** Follow the same procedure as for the traditional putter, except the perfect putter length is not one inch above the hands but from the bottom of the putter head, up the shaft, through the hands, and all the way up until the shaft meets the belly. Belly putters can be from thirty to forty inches long.

▶ **Stand-up length.** This one is easy to measure. You stand up straight while you address a ball. Measure from the ground under the ball to the top of your sternum. Stand-up putter lengths can be anywhere from thirty-seven to sixty-six inches, depending on the fit for you. (See Figure 7.3.)

▶ **Sidesaddle length.** Take your address position without a putter. Measure from the ground under the ball to the bottom of your right armpit. These come in the same length range as the stand-up lengths.

▶ **Split-hand length.** The easiest way to get measured for this putter is to stand up tall and take a measurement from the floor to your belly

7.3. In measuring for a tall putter, you want the butt end of the grip to reach your sternum at your address position.

button. These putters can be from thirty to forty inches long.

Lie

Regardless of the style of putter you use, every putter has a proper lie angle for you. This angle determines how the sole (bottom) of the putter lies on the ground, and this angle can vary from person to person. The importance of this lie angle is that if the proper angle allows the putter to be level to the ground, then the putting stroke will be generally smoother and easier in keeping the putter square to the intended line of putt. The angle is measured from the shaft to the bottom of the putter.

To arrive at the proper lie angle for you, use your putter already fitted for the proper length, and address the ball as you normally would. Have someone assist you and observe whether or not the putter's sole lies level to the ground. If it does, then you already have the proper lie angle. If it does not lie level, then you will need to have the putter adjusted. If the toe of the putter's head is high, you will need to flatten your lie angle enough to make the putter level with the ground. If the heel of the putter's head is high, you will need to make the lie more upright. (See Figure 7.4.)

Loft. Choosing the correct loft angle is an important variable to a putter. The purpose of the loft angle in putting is to allow the putter to get the ball rolling as quickly as possible. If the loft is too much, it will cause the ball to fly. Too little loft will cause the ball to bounce. The loft angle is measured in degrees and is the angle between the putter face and a level surface. Zero degrees of loft is when the putter face is at a 90-degree angle with the surface. A 91-degree angle between the putter face and the surface is considered to be a 1-degree loft. A 92-degree angle equals 2 degrees of loft, and so on.

When choosing the correct loft angle, you will have to consider several things. First is determining the true loft of your putter. You can do this in a workshop with a protractor and base that keeps the face perfectly square. Most club makers have these tools. The true loft of the putter is the angle of the putter face in relation to a level surface. Zero degrees of loft means that the putter face is perpendicular to the surface and facing the horizon. As you add loft, the putter face will be facing above the horizon. Think of a sand wedge that has 56 degrees of loft and how its face is more toward the sky. Most over-the-counter putters come with 2 degrees of loft.

7.4. For the proper lie angle, you want your putter to be flat to the ground at setup, not on the heel or, as shown in this image, set up on the toe.

Second is discovering your effective loft. This measurement is difficult to achieve, because it needs to be measured during a stroke at the moment of impact between the putter and the ball. The reason you need to find the effective loft is because during a stroke, your wrists, arms, body, and ball position all create varying angles that can affect the loft of the putter at the moment of ball-putter impact, and these angles are different for every golfer. I know of only two methods with which you can discover your effective loft: you can record your stroke with a high-speed video camera or you can make an educated guess.

Using high-speed video camera photography, you can position the camera at ground level, focused on the ball from the side. Make your normal putting stroke and capture the shot on film. Take the impact image and measure the angle between the putter face and ground. This will give you the effective loft of your putt. I recommend capturing several images to assure that you create the same loft on each attempt. After measuring the true loft of your putter, you can compare the difference between the true loft and the newly found effective loft. By taking the difference between the two, you will find the proper angle you will need to adjust your putter to create the proper loft for you. Some putter companies actually have this equipment available, and for a fee, you can go and get your putting stroke measured using this method—that is, of course, if you don't already have the fancy equipment yourself.

The second method is to make an educated guess, which can get you as close as possible without the help of high-speed video. For example, if you putt from all neutral setup positions, you keep your body steady and wrists solid during the stroke, and your ball position is a ball forward of center, then the guess would be that your true loft and effective loft will be equal. To guess your effective loft, use the following method. Each of the following factors will add or subtract degrees of loft. For each factor you check yes, add or subtract 1 degree of loft. Use a maximum of +/−3 degrees when using an educated guess. For setup positions:

Hand Position

+1 if hands are ahead of ball position
−1 if hands are behind ball position

Ball Position

+1 if ball is behind center
−1 if ball is forward of center

Weight Distribution

+1 if weight is leaning toward forward foot
−1 if weight is leaning toward rear foot

During the Stroke

+1 if wrist cocks on back stroke but not on through stroke

−1 if wrist does not cock on back stroke and uncocks on through stroke

+1 if weight shifts forward on through stroke

−1 if weight shifts backward on through stroke

With all of that information, you should now have determined the true loft of your putter; combine that with your effective loft, and you can now make the proper adjustments so you have the ideal loft at impact. You might start with a putter with 2 degrees of true loft, but through the stroke and at impact you create different angles and have an effective loft of zero degrees. This would result in your ball bouncing into the ground, creating a very inconsistent putting shot. To choose the correct loft in this example, you should have a putter custom-fit for you with a true loft of 4 degrees, assuming you desire an ideal loft of 2 degrees at impact.

This brings us to the final loft consideration, which is determining the ideal loft for the type of putting green grass that you normally play on. Ideal loft is determined by looking at the type, height, and condition of grass that you are going to be putting on. Different types of grasses require the putter's ideal loft to be different. The ball on the putting green will settle a bit into the grass. The higher and/or thicker the grass, the more the ball will settle. When you stroke a putt, you want your ball to roll on top of the grass. Therefore, with a ball more into the grass, the more ideal loft you will need to get the ball up onto the grass. The shorter and/or less thick the grass, the less ideal loft you will need. For example, a billiard table would require nearly no loft at all. (See Figure 7.5.)

7.5. Here is an image capturing a putter as it strikes the ball. Notice the increased loft of the putter, which means this putter needs adjusting to have the proper impact loft.

Weight

When choosing the proper weight for your putter, you are actually choosing two variables: the true weight and the swing weight.

True Weight. True weight is what the putter weighs statically on a scale. It has an effect on how far the ball can roll and how smooth your putting tempo can be. The ideal true weight of your putter depends on the type and height of the putting green grass that you play on. The basic rule is that the slower the green rolls, the more true weight you will want in your putter. The average weight of most putters sold is 490 grams. This is great for average-speed greens. For slower greens, you might want to use more weight; for faster greens, maybe less.

Swing Weight. Swing weight is the feel of the weight of the club head during a swing. It has an effect on how you feel the control of the putter during a swing. Swing weight is measured on a special scale, which measures the relationship of weight between the grip end of the club and the club head. The more that the weight is positioned toward the club head, the heavier the swing weight and the heavier the club will feel during the swing. The more that the weight is positioned toward the grip end, the lighter the swing weight and the lighter the club will feel during the swing.

The ideal swing weight is a personal choice. Some players like a lighter swing weight, which will give the feeling of more weight in the grip and hands, while some players prefer a heavier swing weight, which gives the club head a weightier feel. It is recommended that a good balance be made between the two extremes. There is a scale that is used to measure swing weight. You can usually find a country club golf professional or a professional club repairer who has a scale that will measure your club's swing weight. The best balanced swing weight for a putter, using a swing weight scale, is a C9. C8 and below is lighter; D1 and above would be heavier. Modifying putter weight is easy to accomplish. The most common method is using lead tape. It can be applied as easily as masking tape and will give you an adjustment of weight. For every one inch of heavy-duty lead tape, you will add about one gram of weight. Modern putter designers now include interchangeable weights so players can alter the weight whenever they choose.

Balance

Choosing the putter's balance has a lot to do with your putting stroke. There are three types of balances in putter design: center (face) balance, toe-heel balance, and no concern for balance.

► **Center (face) balance.** This type of putter balance is ideal for players whose putting stroke keeps the swing path straight back and straight through. This type of balance allows the putter to stay square better with this type of stroke. (See Figure 7.6.)

► **Toe-heel balance.** This type of putter balance is ideal for players whose stroke uses an arcing swing path. This type of balance allows the club head to close in time to a square position at impact.

► **No concern for balance.** This type of putter balance is ideal for players who do not know what their putting stroke is. By using a type of balance that matches your putting stroke, you give yourself a putter that is working with you, as opposed to a putter that requires you to modify your stroke in order to have a chance of working.

7.6. Balance your putter on your finger, and see how the face balances. This particular putter is center (face) balanced because the putter's face is aimed to the sky.

Head Material

Putter heads can be made out of almost any kind of material: metals of all types, plastics, glass, rocks of various kinds, graphite, and so on. The most common material is metal. Steel, zinc, and aluminum are the favorite choices of putter makers. The purpose of the putter head is to impart energy from the moving putter into the stationary golf ball, which causes the golf ball to move. This is why any material could work. The harder the material, the more efficiently the energy is transferred. Some putter designs will incorporate more than one type of material into a single putter head, which can accomplish three different goals: provide an enhanced sensation at impact, improve putter face control, and enable better weight management of the putter. The softer the material, the less energy is transferred. Ideally, you want your putter head material to be consistent with its energy transfer and give a satisfying sensation at putter-ball impact. Some players prefer a harder sensation, while others prefer it to be softer. It is a truly personal decision. There is no benefit of one feel over the other, except that there is a particular feel especially right for you. You will need to experiment to find what you like.

Another consideration when choosing a head material is the type of ball that you play. If you use a golf ball that has a hard feel, you could use a putter with a softer material to adjust to a softer sensation. If you use a soft ball, you might want to use a putter head with a hard material, which would give you a more solid sensation.

Putter Face Material

Putter faces can be made of the same material as the club head, or they can be fitted with an insert of a different material. There are advantages to both. The putter head material may offer you the feel and sensation of impact that you desire, so there would be no need to have an insert in the putter face. If you are looking for a softer feel and you like a metal material for the club head, then a softer insert would be a nice option for the putter face material. Putter designers are also finding that with an advanced type of putter face insert, they can actually get the ball to react in a different way off of the clubface, like achieving a true roll on the ball quicker off of the face, just by altering the makeup and materials of the putter face insert. Some materials that are being used for the inserts are rubber, plastic, softer metals, and combinations of the same. There are new putters on the market that have interchangeable putter faces. This allows the player to alter the feel of the putter face for different playing conditions.

Grip

A grip connects your hands to the putter itself, so it is an important factor to consider. With grips, you will have to consider style, size, weight, material, and color.

► **Style.** The rules of golf allow for some flat edges on a putter grip, which are like cheating when correctly aligned on the putter. These flat edges help to keep the putter more square at impact.

► **Size.** The size of the grip is important for achieving a good feel between your hands and the putter head, as well as to control wrist action during the stroke. Feel is best found in the fingers, so you want as much of your fingers on the putter as you can get. You want a grip size that allows your fingers to wrap around so that the fingertips on the forward hand just touch your palm after you have gripped the putter normally. The size of the grip can influence how the wrists will react during a stroke. The more your hands are closed, the more your wrists feel the need to get into the action, which is not a desired intention. A larger grip will keep the hands more open, in turn helping to keep the wrist action from occurring unnecessarily. Common grip sizes include junior, women's, men's standard, midsize, jumbo, and extra jumbo.

► **Weight.** You need to consider the weight of the grip when choosing one. Some grips can be heavier than others and therefore can cause a change to both true weight and the swing weight of the putter. A heavy grip will create a heavier true weight and a lighter swing weight, and vice versa for a lighter grip.

► **Material.** There are many materials used for the putter's grip, all of which are designed to accomplish only two goals: to provide an area of the putter that the hands can hold and to provide a surface that is comfortable and gives a positive feel for feedback purposes. The materials most commonly used for putter grips are rubber, plastic, leather, cloth tape, wood, and metal. Each has a different feel and has its own pros and cons. This is a personal decision. As long as you are comfortable with the grip, then any material will work fine. Rubber and cloth will have a softer feel, and the others much firmer. Wood and metal will last the longest but are definitely very firm. The most common grip used is the rubber grip. It comes in many forms and of varying hardness but will wear out in two or three years with consistent use.

► **Color.** Color is a very personal decision because it plays no importance to the ability to stroke a quality putt. You will want a color that fits your attitude and personality. Do not pick a color that will make you self-conscious, as this will only distract you and could lead to missed putts.

Shaft Type

There are different types of shafts used in putters. I consider the distinguishing factor when it comes to putter shafts to be how the shafts are bent. The rules allow for the putter shaft to have bends, where all the other clubs must be straight from butt end to tip. The bends of the shaft allow the putter head to be positioned in relation to the shaft at varying points.

In a straight shaft, the shaft is usually placed straight down into the top of the putter head, either at the heel or toward the center of the putter head. This places the front edge of the shaft in line with the putter's face, which creates an onset position. (See Figure 7.7.)

Another type of shaft is the gooseneck shaft, which has a bend at the bottom toward the tip, which allows the shaft to be attached to the top of the putter head. Because of the bend, the shaft bends out in front of the putter face, creating what is called an offset. Some gooseneck shafts can be positioned in a manner that has the shaft bend farther behind the putter, causing an inset putter shaft position, which has the shaft of the putter well behind the putter face.

The third shaft type is the multiple-bend shaft. There are double bends and triple bends. The triple-bend shaft is typically used for the split-hand stroke. No matter the number of bends, you want to make sure that the shaft fits your particular needs.

Choosing the type of shaft depends on the type of onset, inset, or offset position that your stroke prefers. The best way to decide which you need is to determine where you like your hands to be at impact with the ball. If you like your hands in front of the ball at impact, then an offset putter shaft would be appropriate. If you prefer your hands to return above the ball, then an onset shaft would be correct. And if it works best for you to have your hands return behind the ball, then an inset shaft would work best.

7.7.
Different putters and their shafts are represented here. From left to right: an onset center shafted putter, an offset modified blade, a gooseneck mallet, and a triple bend shaft ideal for the split-hand stroke.

Shaft Material

There are three different types of materials that are normally used to make putter shafts: metal (aluminum and steel), graphite, and wood. Shafts are necessary in that they connect your hands atop the grip to the putter head. Most great putters nowadays are made with steel shafts. A good steel shaft will flex just the right amount and provide just enough vibration to give the player a good feel of his or her stroke and the appropriate feedback needed to keep the stroke at its best.

8

PUT YOUR PUTTING STROKE
TO THE TEST

All great players test their games quite often to prove to themselves how good they are and to make sure that they are not straying away from what has given them success. It is important to know how proficient you currently are at creating consistency, controlling direction and distance, and implementing the mental skills, so your practice time is focused and precise. The following tests are designed to provide you with valuable feedback about your putting game and stroke. After completing the tests, you will know exactly what skills problems you have and what exactly you need to work on to improve your putting game and stroke. Take the tests in order, and note your results. Following each test, examine your results to determine the probable causes of your errors. This will help you formulate your plan of improvement. In the future, by taking the tests again, you will know how far you have progressed.

1 THE ALIGNMENT TEST

This test is designed to assess your ability to properly align yourself and the putter toward a target. Aiming correctly at your target is essential.

If you are not aimed at your target to begin with, your chances of following the putting laws and holing the putt are really poor. The most common error from alignment is poor direction control. If you consistently miss on the same side of the hole, or your putts are just missing the edges of the hole, poor alignment may be the problem.

Items You Need to Take the Test

> Golf ball
> Putter
> Pointer (club shaft or quarter-inch dowel)
> Target (a hole on the green, a coin, or another golf ball)

The Test

1. Place your golf ball ten feet from your target on a fairly flat surface.
2. Address the ball and take dead aim for the target.
3. Before you move or wiggle the club head, have an assistant move the ball out of the way and then take the pointer and place it perpendicular to the putter's face. This will show where you have aimed for the most accurate feedback. You must not see how you have done until the test is over.
4. Have your assistant take notes as to whether the aim was dead-on straight or to the left or right of the target.
5. Repeat this nine times.

Having an assistant track the results, without you knowing how well you aimed on each attempt, will give you the best information at the conclusion of the test. (See Figure 8.1.) If you happen to see that you missed left or right, you might make adjustments based on that information, and you will not have the proper results that will help your putting game. The goal is for the results to be determined by your normal attempts, not by attempts made by reacting to the previous shot's result.

Examine Your Results

Did you miss most to the right? If so, one of the following potential problems in key areas is most likely the cause:

► **Grip.** Too tight and the grip pressure or the palms have rotated left of square.

► **Eyes.** Positioned inside the ball position, or the dominant eye is positioned forward of the ball's position.

► **Stance of feet, hips, or shoulders.** Aligned to the right of the target line.

► **Hands and arms.** Positioned too close to the body, or the forearms are held too close to the body.

► **Balance.** Either body weight is too far back on the heels or too much weight is on the forward foot.

► **Posture.** Standing too upright.

► **Ball.** Positioned too far back in the stance or too far away from the body.

► **Aiming.** Not visualizing the line.

► **Putter.** Either the lie angle is too flat, there's too much loft, the shaft is too long, or the grip has been installed incorrectly.

8.1. With help from an assistant, chart the accuracy of your alignment routine. This example is misaligned to the left.

Did you miss most to the left?

► **Grip.** Too loose with the grip pressure, or the palms have rotated right of square.

► **Eyes.** Positioned outside the ball position, or the dominant eye is positioned rearward of the ball position.

► **Stance of feet, hips, or shoulders.** Aligned to the left of the target line.

► **Hands.** Positioned too far from the body, or the forearms are too far from the body.

► **Balance.** Too much weight on the toes or the rear foot.

► **Posture.** Too bent over.

► **Ball.** Position too far forward in the stance or too close to the body.

► **Aiming.** Not visualizing the line.

► **Putter.** Either the lie angle is too upright, there's not enough loft, the shaft is too short, or the grip has been incorrectly installed.

Did you miss a similar amount left and right?

► **Grip.** Inconsistent or changing grip pressure during the stroke.

► **Aim.** Not focusing clearly on the target.

► **Ball.** Position is inconsistent in its placement from shot to shot.

► **Balance.** Inconsistent distribution of weight from shot to shot.

► **Routine.** Inconsistent between shots. Not applying proper alignment checks.

Did you align all straight? It would seem then that you have already mastered alignment.

2 THE SWEET SPOT TEST

This test will show how consistent you are in following the putting law of striking the putter's sweet spot. The purpose of consistently striking the sweet spot is so that the energy you create with the back stroke is most efficiently transferred into the golf ball. This efficient energy transfer is needed for you to have control over your feel for distance. A missed sweet spot will also cause a ball not to roll correctly, and makes for poor direction control. The most common error from missing the sweet spot is having both very long and very short misses throughout a round of golf. (See Figure 8.2.)

Items You Need to Take the Test

> Golf ball
> Putter
> Impact marking agent (face impact tape, baby powder)

The Test

1. Place your marking agent correctly. Impact tape is stuck to the putter face. Baby powder is placed on the back of the ball, preferably to fill only one dimple.
2. Make a stroke at the ball to a target of your choice. The distance can be anywhere from three to ten feet.
3. An assistant should make note of the impact position on the putter face: center, left, or right.
4. Repeat nine times.

8.2. By checking your sweet spot contact with baby powder, you can learn where some of your putting problems may lie. This example shows the impact position toward the toe.

Examine Your Results

Did most results miss toward the heel? One of the following is probably the cause:

▶ **Grip.** Too tight with too much grip pressure, or the putter's grip is held too much in the fingers.
▶ **Ball.** Too close to the body or too far back in the stance.

- ▶ **Eyes.** Positioned too far outside the ball's position, or the dominant eye is too far back behind the ball.
- ▶ **Posture.** Bent over more than is needed.
- ▶ **Knees.** Too much bend.
- ▶ **Balance.** Too much weight on the toes, or leaning too much on the forward foot. Or possibly the weight has moved toward the forward foot during the stroke.
- ▶ **Stance.** Too wide.
- ▶ **Hands.** Too close to the body at setup, or there is too much angle between the forearms and putter shaft, or the hands may have pushed away from the body on the back stroke.
- ▶ **Swing path.** Pushed outside the proper line on the back stroke.
- ▶ **Putter.** Shaft is too long for your stroke.

Did most miss toward the toe?

- ▶ **Grip.** Pressure is too loose.
- ▶ **Ball.** Positioned too far from the body or too far forward in the stance.
- ▶ **Eyes.** Positioned too much to the inside of the ball, or the dominant eye is positioned too much ahead of the ball.
- ▶ **Posture.** Too upright.
- ▶ **Balance.** Too much weight on the heels, leaning too much on the back foot, or weight has moved toward the back foot during the stroke.
- ▶ **Stance.** Too narrow.
- ▶ **Hands.** Too far from the body at setup, or the hands pulled too close to the body on the back stroke.
- ▶ **Swing path.** Pulled inside the proper line on the back stroke.
- ▶ **Putter.** Shaft is too short for your stroke.

Did most miss high on the face?

- ► **Ball.** Positioned too far back in the stance.
- ► **Angle of attack.** Too steep.
- ► **Shoulders.** Tilted more forward than needed.
- ► **Hands.** Set too far ahead of the ball. The arms have lifted up too high on the back stroke. The arms have bent on the back stroke.
- ► **Pivot point.** Positioned ahead of the ball, or has moved ahead of the ball during the stroke.

Did most miss low on the face?

- ► **Ball.** Positioned too far forward in the stance.
- ► **Angle of attack.** Too shallow and the putter is too high off of the ground.
- ► **Shoulders.** Too much tilt.
- ► **Hands.** Set up behind the ball.
- ► **Arms.** Bent on back stroke and never straightened back out.
- ► **Pivot point.** Too far behind the ball on setup, or has moved there during the stroke.

Were all hit on the sweet spot? If so, then today you were spot-on. Check again at another time to make sure that you really are that consistent in hitting the sweet spot.

3 THE FACE TEST

This test will determine how accurately you return your putter face at impact and how well you follow the square putter face putting law. If you have mastered alignment prior to the stroke, then this is an essential piece to get correct if you want your ball to go where you have directed it. The common errors of an incorrect putter face position are pulls and pushes. (See Figure 8.3.)

8.3. Without a square putter face at impact, you are likely to either push or pull your putt.

Items You Need to Take the Test

Two golf balls or a three-quarter-inch PVC pipe three inches long
Putter

The Test

1. Place the two golf balls side by side or the PVC pipe on the putting green or a similar surface.
2. Align the putter face squarely to the balls or PVC pipe.
3. Make a stroke to contact the putter face squarely with the golf balls or the pipe.
4. Make note of the reaction of the golf balls or pipe. Golf balls: both roll together, left shoots ahead of the right, or right shoots

ahead of the left. PVC pipe: rolls straight, spins left, or spins right.

5. Repeat nine times.

Examine Your Results

If you used the golf ball method, did the left ball move out ahead of the right ball for most of your results? Or with the pipe method, did most spin right?

- ► **Clubface.** Closed, or turned too much to the left.
- ► **Grip.** Closed, or palms are turned too much to the right.
- ► **Stance.** Closed, or aimed too much to the right.
- ► **Hands.** Set up too far from the body.
- ► **Arms.** Rotated to a closed position, or twisted right of parallel.
- ► **Swing path.** Swung outside the proper line on the back stroke.
- ► **Shoulders.** Closed, or the left shoulder is pushed ahead toward the ball, while the rear shoulder goes back.
- ► **Eyes.** Dominant eye is positioned too far behind the ball's position.
- ► **Balance.** Weight is too much on the back foot, or too much is on the toes.
- ► **Pivot point.** Positioned too far behind the ball's position.
- ► **Ball.** Positioned too far forward or too far away from the body.
- ► **Putter.** Too long, or the lie angle is too upright for the stroke.

Did the right ball move out ahead of the left ball for most of your results? Or if you used the pipe method, did most spin left?

- ► **Grip.** Open, or the palms are turned too much to the left.
- ► **Stance.** Open, or aimed too much to the left of the intended line.

- ► **Hands.** Too close to the body.
- ► **Arms.** Rotated to an open position, or twisted left of parallel during the stroke.
- ► **Swing path.** Inside the proper line on the back stroke.
- ► **Clubface.** Open, or turned too much to the right.
- ► **Shoulders.** Open, or rear shoulder has pushed ahead of the forward shoulder.
- ► **Eyes.** Dominant eye is positioned too much ahead of the ball.
- ► **Balance.** Too much weight is positioned on the forward foot, or too much is on the heels.
- ► **Pivot point.** Positioned too far ahead of the ball.
- ► **Ball.** Positioned too far back in the stance or too close to the body.
- ► **Putter.** Too short, or the lie angle is too flat.

Were the results mixed?

- ► **Grip.** Inconsistent positioning or the grip pressure changed during the stroke.
- ► **Aim.** Not focusing clearly on the intended line or the golf balls or pipe.
- ► **Ball.** Position is inconsistent in its placement from shot to shot.
- ► **Balance.** Inconsistent distribution of weight from shot to shot.
- ► **Routine.** Inconsistent between shots. Not applying proper alignment checks.

4 THE CRAYON TEST

This test will show you the angle of attack of your putter on the through stroke. (See Figure 8.4.) The angle of attack, one of the five putting laws, is the up-and-down path that the putter travels throughout a stroke. Ideally, you want your putter to be traveling level to the ground at impact.

This test will show you where your putter levels out. The most common error with a problematic angle of attack is controlling distance.

Items You Need to Take the Test

> 8½-by-11-inch piece of paper
> Putter
> Tape
> Marking device (crayons or dull golf pencil)

The Test

1. Draw a golf ball–sized circle on the middle of the paper.
2. Tape the paper to a hard floor surface.
3. Tape the marking device to the putter face with the writing end sticking out about a quarter of an inch below the putter.
4. Address the drawn golf ball with the marking device touching the paper.
5. Make a stroke at the drawn ball.
6. Repeat six times.

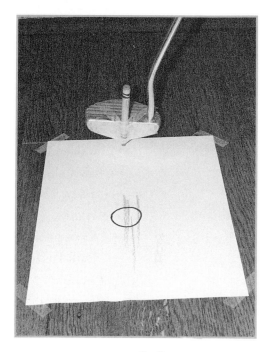

8.4. A good angle of attack lets you roll your putts smoothly. Use this test to determine your angle of attack.

Examine Your Results

Were most of the lines longer after the ball?

- ► **Grip.** Pressure is too tight.
- ► **Balance.** Weight is positioned too much on the forward foot.
- ► **Shoulders.** Do not have enough tilt.
- ► **Body.** There is movement toward the target during the stroke.
- ► **Hands.** Too far pressed forward at setup.
- ► **Wrists.** Too cocked.

- ► **Pivot point.** Too much ahead of the ball's position.
- ► **Ball.** Positioned too far back in the stance.

Were most of the lines longer before the ball?

- ► **Grip.** Pressure is too loose.
- ► **Balance.** Weight is positioned too much on the back foot.
- ► **Shoulders.** Too much tilt.
- ► **Body.** There is movement away from the target during the stroke.
- ► **Hands.** Positioned behind the ball at setup.
- ► **Pivot point.** Positioned too much behind the ball.
- ► **Ball.** Positioned too far forward in the stance.

Were there no lines? Or were the lines very short? The lines should be about four inches in length. Lines that are only two inches or less are considered very short.

- ► **Grip.** Pressure is too tight.
- ► **Balance.** Weight is too much on the heels.
- ► **Shoulders.** Too much tilt.
- ► **Body.** Lifted during the stroke.
- ► **Arms.** Too bent at setup, or are bending during the stroke.
- ► **Posture.** Too upright at setup, or is becoming more upright during the stroke.
- ► **Pivot point.** Lifting during the stroke.
- ► **Putter.** Shaft is too short for your stroke.

Was the crayon ripping the paper? If this is happening, then the angle of attack is much too steep.

- ► **Grip.** Pressure is too tight.
- ► **Balance.** Weight is positioned too much on the toes.

- ► **Shoulders.** Do not have enough tilt.
- ► **Body.** Dropping during the stroke.
- ► **Arms.** Too bent at setup, or are bending during the stroke.
- ► **Wrists.** Excessive movement on the back stroke.
- ► **Posture.** Too upright at setup, is becoming more upright during the back stroke, or is lowering during the down stroke.
- ► **Pivot point.** Lifting during the back stroke.
- ► **Putter.** Shaft is too short for your stroke.

Were all your lines ideal? The ideal lines will be about four inches long and should begin two inches before the back edge of the ball. If all of your lines are ideal, then you have mastered your angle of attack.

5 THE SWING PATH TEST

This test will determine how well you follow the swing path putting law through a stroke. Whether you are a straight-back straight-through player or an inside-square-inside player, this will show you how well you repeat your path. (See Figure 8.5.) The path is an important piece of the stroke because it, along with the face position, helps to determine the direction the ball will begin. An error in the swing path is the most common cause of pulls and pushes.

Items You Need to Take the Test

Golf ball
Putter
Twenty golf tees

The Test

1. Arrange half of the tees two inches apart in a straight line.
2. Arrange the remaining tees two inches apart in a straight line parallel to the first, with enough room between the two lines to

8.5. Most players assume they know what path they are attempting. This test will help you to learn how consistent your path actually is.

allow the putter head to fit with half an inch of room on either side.

3. Place the ball in the center of the tees.
4. Make a stroke at the ball.
5. Note which tees you have knocked down.
6. Rearrange the tees and repeat nine times.

Examine Your Results

By noting the tees that you knock down during a stroke, you can determine the path that your putter is moving during the stroke. This information will be vital to help you in learning how to improve your swing path during a putt.

If you are attempting a straight-back straight-through path, there should not be any tees knocked down. If the tees on the outside are being knocked down, then it could be because of one of the following reasons:

► **Grip.** Too tight.
► **Balance.** Weight is positioned too much on the toes.
► **Stance.** Not parallel to the intended line.
► **Eyes.** Positioned outside the ball, or are not level.
► **Shoulders.** Turning during the stroke, instead of rocking.
► **Ball.** Positioned too far forward in the stance.
► **Posture.** Too bent over.
► **Pivot point.** Positioned behind the ball's position.
► **Arms.** Too much bend.

If you are attempting a straight-back straight-through path and the tees on the inside are being knocked down, then the cause may be one of the following:

► **Grip.** Too loose, or perhaps the grip is positioned too much in the fingers.
► **Balance.** Weight is positioned on the heels.
► **Stance.** Not parallel to the intended line.
► **Eyes.** Positioned inside of the ball's position, or are not level.
► **Shoulders.** Turning during the stroke, instead of rocking.
► **Ball.** Positioned too far back in the stance.
► **Posture.** Too upright.
► **Pivot point.** Positioned ahead of the ball.
► **Arms.** Too much bend, or too much rotation during the stroke.

If you are attempting an inside-square-inside path, then only the first or second end tees on both ends should be knocked down. The number knocked down will depend on your particular arc. If the tees on the outside are being knocked down, then the following are probable reasons:

- ► **Grip.** Too tight.
- ► **Balance.** The weight is on the toes.
- ► **Stance.** Not square.
- ► **Eyes.** Positioned outside of the ball's position.
- ► **Shoulders.** Closed at address.
- ► **Ball.** Positioned too close to the body, or positioned too far forward in the stance.
- ► **Posture.** Too bent over, or is bent down during the stroke.
- ► **Pivot point.** Positioned ahead of the ball.
- ► **Arms.** Rotated closed at address, or are not rotating during the stroke.

If you are attempting an inside-square-inside path, and more tees then the end one or two tees from the inside line are being knocked down, then the following are probable reasons:

- ► **Grip.** Too loose.
- ► **Balance.** Weight is positioned on the heels.
- ► **Stance.** Not square.
- ► **Eyes.** Positioned inside of the ball's position.
- ► **Shoulders.** Open at address.
- ► **Ball.** Positioned too far from the body, or is too far back in the stance.
- ► **Posture.** Too upright, or is becoming more upright during the stroke.
- ► **Pivot point.** Positioned behind the ball's position.
- ► **Arms.** Rotated open at setup, or too much rotation during stroke.

6 THE FEEL FOR DISTANCE TEST

This test is to determine your feel for controlling distance and how well you obey the club head speed law. Touch is an innate sensation that helps us sense what our bodies need to do to create a specific result. In putting, we need our bodies to feel what it takes to roll a putt a specific distance.

Items You Need to Take the Test

> Golf ball
> Putter

The Test

1. Find a level area of a putting green.
2. Place your golf ball fifteen feet from the hole.
3. Address your ball.
4. Stare at the hole so your eyes relay a distance message to your brain.
5. Close your eyes.
6. Stroke your putt with your eyes still closed.
7. Once you believe the ball has stopped, open your eyes to see where it has landed. (See Figure 8.6.)
8. Repeat nine times.

Examine Your Results

Were most attempts past the hole? If they were all within eighteen inches past the hole, then your distance control is fantastic. If they were farther than eighteen inches, then you should look at the following areas for improvement:

8.6. With your eyes closed, you will have to trust your feel to control the distance.

- ► **Tempo.** Too slow on the back stroke.
- ► **Grip.** Not maintaining the same pressure throughout the stroke.
- ► **Stroke.** Length is too long on the back stroke or is too long on the follow-through.
- ► **Acceleration.** Too fast during the down stroke, or not maintaining a pendulum-type motion.
- ► **Arms.** Bent during the stroke.
- ► **Wrists.** Adding power during the stroke.
- ► **Body.** Moving during the stroke.

Were most attempts short of the hole?

- ► **Tempo.** Too slow throughout the stroke, or too fast on the back stroke.
- ► **Grip.** Not maintaining the same pressure throughout the stroke, is too tight, or is not set up in a square position.
- ► **Stroke length.** Too short on the back stroke, or is too short both back and through.
- ► **Sweet spot.** Missed.
- ► **Angle of attack.** Either too steep or too shallow.
- ► **Swing path.** Crooked.
- ► **Acceleration.** Slowing down on the down stroke (decelerating), or stopping too quickly after the ball is struck.
- ► **Arms, wrists, and body.** Too tight, or are in improper setup positions.
- ► **Stance.** Not set up properly.
- ► **Balance.** Off at the setup, or lost during the stroke.
- ► **Ball.** Not positioned in its proper location for your stroke.
- ► **Eyes.** Not in their proper setup position.

Was there an even mix of long and short attempts?

- **Tempo.** Inconsistent, or either too slow or too fast on the back stroke.
- **Grip.** Inconsistent between shots, or the pressure is changing during the stroke.
- **Stroke length.** Inconsistent from shot to shot.
- **Sweet spot.** Inconsistently struck.
- **Angle of attack.** Either too steep or too shallow.
- **Swing path.** Inconsistent in its direction.
- **Acceleration.** Too fast on the down stroke, slowing down at impact, or speeding up unnecessarily after impact.
- **Arms, wrists, and body.** All may have excessive movement.

7 THE PENDULUM TEST

All great putting strokes move the putter in a pendulum-like motion. This motion helps to create a rhythm and helps to enhance a player's feel for distance. This test is designed to check for an ideal pendulum motion length, by making sure that the putter head moves the same length on both the back stroke and the follow-through. (See Figure 8.7.) A good pendulum motion is an indicator that you have obeyed all of the putting laws.

Items You Need to Take the Test

Six golf tees
Six markers (pennies or flat ball markers)
Golf ball
Putter

The Test

1. Place tees in a row two inches apart.
2. Place the golf ball far enough in front of the lead tee to allow room for the putter's head.

8.7. To effectively control your distance, you want to make sure your pendulum is swinging the same length both on the back stroke and the follow-through.

3. Line the markers in a row, spaced two inches apart from each other, in front of the ball.
4. Attempt a six-foot length putt, and hold your finish position.
5. See which ball marker your putter face has finished over.
6. Count the number of tees knocked down.

Examine Your Results

If you knocked down the same number of tees as the number of markers your putter face finished over, then you have an ideal length of pendulum motion. For most greens, the length of the back stroke will be about six inches for a six-foot putt. A general rule is that for every one foot of putt, the pendulum should move one inch behind, and one inch past the ball.

Did you knock down more tees on the back stroke than the number of markers on the follow-through?

- ► **Grip.** Too loose.
- ► **Swing path.** Has been forced into staying too straight back on the back stroke.
- ► **Tempo.** Too fast on back stroke, or too slow on the down stroke.
- ► **Wrists.** Excessive movement.
- ► **Body.** Movement during the back stroke.
- ► **Pivot point.** Too far behind the ball's position.
- ► **Balance.** Too much weight on the rear foot.
- ► **Posture.** Too bent over.
- ► **Shoulders.** Too much tilt.

Did you stop over more markers on the follow-through than the tees you knocked down on the back stroke?

- ► **Grip.** Too tight.
- ► **Tempo.** Too slow on the back stroke, or too fast on the down stroke.
- ► **Wrists.** Excessive movement during the down stroke.
- ► **Body.** Movement during the down stroke.
- ► **Pivot point.** Positioned too far ahead of the ball's position.
- ► **Balance.** Too much weight on the forward foot.
- ► **Posture.** Too upright.
- ► **Shoulders.** Need more tilt.

8 THE MENTAL QUOTIENT (MQ) TEST

The mental skills are largely left to develop on their own, without specific practice techniques to encourage their development. This test will give you insight as to how well you use your mental skills.

Items You Need to Take the Test

A pencil

The Test

Answer the following multiple-choice questions by circling your answers:

1. After addressing your ball to putt, are you (a) often, (b) sometimes, or (c) never worried that you will miss the shot?
2. How many putters do you own? (a) four or more, (b) two to four, (c) one
3. What kind of putter do you consider yourself to be? (a) poor, (b) OK, (c) great

4. How many times during eighteen holes do you change your putting swing thought? (a) never, (b) one to three times, (c) more than three times

5. Do you warm up on the practice green prior to play? (a) always, (b) sometimes, (c) never

6. When you miss a putt, where would you prefer it to be? (a) does not matter—a miss is a miss, (b) two inches away missed on either side of the hole, (c) eighteen inches away missed on the high side

7. Do you (a) often, (b) sometimes, (c) never, while on the putting green, have a discussion or trade a joke?

8. Do you (a) often, (b) sometimes, (c) never, while on the putting green, think about how well or poorly your hole or round is progressing?

9. Do you (a) often, (b) sometimes, (c) never, while on the putting green, think about what may be going on at home or work?

Examine Your Results

1. **If you answered "often," then you are not prepared well enough to make the shot.** You need to improve your confidence levels. Review your strategies and your preshot routines. You should never attempt a putt unless you are confident that you have prepared to give it your best attempt. If you do not think you can make it before you even try, then you most likely will not. If you answered "sometimes," then make it a rule never to strike a putt unless you are confident that it will have a chance to go in. It just takes a little extra preparation time to make sure you are confident in what you are about to do. If you answered that you are never worried, then you are very confident or you are overly confident, which can lead to lack of preparation and loss of routine. Be careful not to let your confidence disrupt your good routines.

2. **If you own four or more putters, then you need to get properly fit for one (assuming that if you have been already, the custom club would be the only one you'd need).** Make sure that when you do, you have a stroke that fits you, and make sure your mechanics are appropriate for your stroke and putter. If you only own two to four putters, then hopefully you've had some success with one or two of them. Determine which has given you the best success over the years, find out what makes that putter particularly unique for your stroke, and make sure it fits you. If you only have one, chances are that it is very close to a perfect fit. Correct the one or two faulty variables in the putter, and the putter will probably become a long-time best friend and a true confidence booster.

3. **If you consider yourself to be a poor putter, then you need to build your confidence.** Understand the need for a proper fit in stroke and equipment. Learn the laws of putting and the mechanics that obey the laws, and practice properly to build your confidence. If you consider yourself to be an OK putter, then you are simply missing an element that will push you toward being great. Find the missing piece by examining your equipment, your mechanics, your green-reading skills, and your mental skills. The missing piece is in there somewhere. If you consider yourself to be a great putter, then you better have the statistics to back up the claim. It is good to be confident in your abilities, but do not let false confidence prevent you from trying to be even better.

4. **If you change your putting swing thought more than three times during eighteen holes, then you are not practicing correctly.** Proper practice will narrow down your specific problem areas. With a problem area found, you only need, at most, a couple of swing thoughts to repair the problem. If you are trying more than three thoughts in eighteen holes, then you are experimenting on the course. Experimenting on

the course will never lead to improvement worthy enough to outweigh all the misses during the experimentation. Experimenting also leads to poor confidence levels, especially if there are no signs of improvement. If you only change your swing thought one to three times in eighteen holes, then you know that you have a problem, and you at least have narrowed down your thoughts that help to solve the problem. By also limiting the number of thoughts, you will be able to gain enough feedback to learn if the swing thoughts were actually effective or not. If you never have a swing thought, then either you are the greatest unconscious putter of all time or you just do not know what to think. Even if your swing thought for the rest of your life is to put the ball in the hole, you need some kind of thought that prevents the subconscious from allowing negative thoughts.

5. **If you never warm up prior to play, then you are sacrificing a great opportunity to begin green reading, secure your day's swing thought, and loosen up the muscles and mind to prepare for the first hole.** If you use the first hole as a warm-up, then you are just not going to have the mind-set of a great putter. Great putters want to have a one-putt on every green. If you are busy warming up on the first green, then you are not mentally or physically prepared to one-putt, unless you have knocked it to two feet from the fairway. In this case, your warm-up will not happen until the second hole. If you occasionally warm up prior to play, then all you need to do to improve your putting game is to warm up every time. By not warming up every time, you cannot be consistent. Consistency is the mark of a great putter. Warm up every time and create consistency. If you warm up every time, congratulations. That is the kind of putter I like to see.

6. **If it does not matter to you where you miss your putts, then you are not reading the greens properly.** If you prefer to miss the hole on the high side, even if it is eighteen inches too high, then you

are overreading the greens to make sure that you look like a pro. It is commonly said that pros miss on the high side of the hole, whereas amateurs miss on the low side. If a pro always missed, but only on the high side, there would not be a lot of money made. Missing is one thing; purposely missing to look better just does not make you better. If you answered two inches away on either side, then I like your thinking. You are telling yourself that you want the ball to go in the hole, but if you do miss, then your distance control was perfect, and you walk out of the hole with a simple tap-in.

7. **If, while on the putting green, you often have discussions or trade jokes, then you are not concentrating enough on your green reading.** You want your concentration to be at its best while on the putting green waiting for your turn to putt. A lack of concentration can cause mental errors in your putting game. If you sometimes trade jokes, then your routine is being interrupted. It is never good to interrupt your routine. This can cause errors in green reading and a shift in your normal tempo. If you are prone to telling jokes, then make sure you do so between holes, when there is not as much at stake. If you never discuss or tell jokes on the greens, then you have learned when and where on the course to have your fun. Holing putts is great fun. Telling a joke on your way to the next tee after sinking a putt for par or better—well, that is just priceless.

8. **If you often or even only sometimes think about how well or poorly your round is going on the putting green, then your concentration is suffering.** You need to employ a strategy to combat this error. You should never think about the overall outcome but should instead focus on the next shot, which on the putting green is the next putt. Go through your normal routine when you have controlled your poor mind-set if you want to be a great putter. The only way to conquer this problem is to avoid thinking about your round on the putting

green. A good strategy and rock-solid routines are the way to stay in the present.

9. **If you have thoughts in your head, other than putting routines, while on the putting green, then you have a concentration problem.** Again, you will need a strategy to combat these thoughts. Sometimes what may be going on at home or work is very important. If this is the case, then you should probably be off the course taking care of that problem. If the problem is minor, then a good strategy to combat the interruptive thoughts will work. When the mind is in order away from the course, you will be able to keep your mind concentrated while on the putting green. If you never think about what is happening off the course, thank your lucky stars. I have had to develop a good strategy to combat my busy thoughts from off the golf course.

9 THE PUTT FOR DOUGH TEST

The single most important distance to master in putting is the three-footer. This is true because, for one, you face this length putt quite often in a round of golf and also because a solid three-footer putting stroke shows you how well you are obeying all of the putting laws. You will never be known as a great putter if you miss this length very often.

Items You Need to Take the Test

> Golf ball
> Putter
> Marker (golf tee)

The Test

1. Place your ball three feet from a hole on a level putting surface and mark the position with a golf tee.

2. Address your ball.
3. Stroke the putt.
4. Repeat until you miss. Keep track of how many putts you make in a row.

Examine Your Results

One hundred in a row, without a miss: tour quality

Fifty in a row, without a miss: amateur champ

Twenty-five in a row, without a miss: club champ

Ten in a row, without a miss: it's a start

Fewer than ten in a row: need more practice

10 THE BEAT THE BEST TEST

To be the best, you need to beat the best. This test is designed to challenge all of your putting skills in one difficult test. Passing this test could put you on your way to becoming a putting legend.

Items You Need to Take the Test

Six golf balls

Ten golf tees

Putter

The Test

1. On a practice putting green, use a hole with at least thirty feet of length for putting. Some slope and break is OK.
2. Place the tees (no more than seven) behind the hole in a semi-circle with an eighteen-inch radius, about eight inches apart and with the side tees even with the front of the hole.
3. Place a single tee as a marker at ten feet, twenty feet, and thirty feet.

4. Starting at the ten-foot marker, putt all six balls with the objective of having them finish either in the hole or within the semicircle of tees.

5. Once a ball strikes a tee or fails to land in the target area, the test is over.

6. If all six balls are successful at ten feet, retrieve the balls, move to the twenty-foot marker, and continue. When all six balls are successful at twenty feet, move to the thirty-foot marker.

7. The object of the test is to successfully land all eighteen shots with as many as possible in the hole, or at least within the semicircle.

Examine Your Results

Hole out all eighteen: legend of putting

Land all eighteen, with at least half hole outs: putting master

Land all eighteen: great putter

Land at least twelve: good putter

Land at least six: fair putter

Land less than six: try again

Now that you have taken all of the tests, you should have learned exactly where you stand in regard to your putting game. Incorporate this knowledge into your practice routine and before too long, you will notice a definitive improvement to your putting.

9

FIXING FAULTS WITH PRACTICE DRILLS AND TRAINING AIDS

For many years, good players and teachers have been using practice drills and training aids as tools to help fix their faults and master their putting game. Just look at the practice green at a professional golf event. You will see players using many different approaches to help them work on their putting games. One of the problems many amateur players have is figuring out which drills and aids to use to solve their unique problems and help them to improve their putting. It is important to know that practicing needs to be more than just going to the practice putting green and striking putts for a little while. An effective practice routine will have you properly spending your time developing and reinforcing the skills that you need to improve your putting. All successful tour pros have effective practice routines. (See Figure 9.1.)

If you are going to have an effective practice, you need to create an efficient routine that will address your faults, improve your putting skills, and incorporate those skills into a playing situation. Some practice routines may last fifteen minutes, while others may last hours. It all

9.1. Here is Vijay Singh using a putting track training aid to work on his swing path and perfect his stroke.

depends on what is effective for you. I have a method to help you design your own practice routine. Follow my proven four-step system each and every time you practice, and before long you will have developed a solid practice routine.

The first step is determining what mechanic to work on. The three remaining steps feature a series of practice drills and training aids, of which you will choose the most suitable for your particular needs. I'll review the drills to help you decide which will work best for you and in doing so give you the most extensive and beneficial practice sessions possible.

STEP 1: WORK ON YOUR MECHANICS

Always begin your practice with a focus on your putting mechanics. The purpose of starting this way is to make sure that your mechanics are correct before you work on the skills that will incorporate them. You want to make sure that you have corrected any problem mechanics and have eliminated any bad habits formed since your last game or practice. If you practice your skills with faulty mechanics, you will have a harder time achieving success with the drills and the training aids, and you will be ingraining faulty mechanics into your stroke. Review the list that follows to help you figure out the cause of your particular fault. If there is more than one fault, unless you determine that each is caused by the same exact problem, attack them independently.

1. Determine which skill is most affected. Is it distance control or direction control?
2. Determine which of the laws is most problematic. Is it sweet spot, swing path, angle of attack, club head speed, or square putter face?
3. Determine which of your body mechanics is most likely to blame for the problem. Try to narrow down to a particular body part: hands, arms, shoulders, legs, hips, or torso.
4. Determine the exact piece of the body part that is most likely causing the putting error.

Once you have determined the culprit body part, you need to determine the swing thought you are going to use to improve the mechanic. Here is an example of a direction-control fault:

I found I was missing putts to the right of the hole. First I examined my stroke to determine which of the laws I was most likely violating. I decided it was the putter face not remaining square. To help me figure out what body part could be causing

9.2. The legs-out drill forces you into a centered weight balance and eliminates unwanted lower body movement.

the fault, I pulled out my two-ball training aid and started stroking some putts to see if I could evaluate the mechanics problems that were causing my putter face not to remain square. After a few strokes I realized my knees were moving while I made the stroke. My swing thought was then to keep my knees steady. I practiced the legs-out drill, which helped me and my muscles to keep my knees steady. (See Figure 9.2.)

Sometimes it is difficult to self-diagnose your mechanical issues. As a teacher and player, I know there are times when I cannot quickly determine the cause of a fault I am having, so I will look to my friends and fellow professionals to help me locate what I cannot see. It never hurts to have an extra set of eyes working on the problem, especially if the extra eyes know what they are looking for and how to properly convey what they see.

STEP 2: PRACTICE YOUR DIRECTION-CONTROL SKILL

This step is where we apply drills and training aids to work on and improve your putting direction-control skill. Choose one or more of the following drills and training aids to improve your direction-control skills. I have found that the distance-control skill practice is much more effective after a good direction-control skill practice. Whenever possible, choose drills and aids that will also help improve your mechanical faults. Once you have confidence in your mechanics and are controlling the starting direction of your putts, you will be ready to move to step 3.

9.3. If you miss, you must start over.

Drills

► **Three-footer drill.** Putt on a straight and level area. Putt into the hole a number of times in a row. If you miss at any time, you must start over at one. (See Figure 9.3.) It is common for the great putters to do fifty or a hundred in a row.

► **Around-the-hole drill.** Some say that Dave Pelz created this drill, while others believe it was Jackie Burke. It does not matter, because it is a simple and very effective drill to use, one that Phil Mickelson uses to master his short putts. Place six or eight balls in a circle around the hole, each three feet away. Putt each one into the hole in succession. If you miss, replace the balls and start over. The goal is to make

If you get around the circle without a miss, replace the balls and then go in the opposite direction.

each one without missing. (See Figure 9.4.) This is a good practice for three-foot breaking putts. Choose a hole with a slight break.

► **Arc drill.** Address your ball as normal. Place your putter so the ball is adjacent to the heel of the putter. Stroke the putt and hit the ball on the sweet spot. First try the putt while looking at the ball. Next try with your eyes looking at the target, and feel the path of the putter creating an arc. Finally, try with your eyes closed.

► **Between-the-tees drill.** Place two tees about three inches apart from each other, and place your ball three feet away. The object is to hit a certain number between the tees, with your expected number rising as you progress. This is a good drill if your straight putting is an issue. (See Figure 9.5.)

▶ **Bump-the-ball drill.** Place a ball on the green. Place another ball three feet from it. The object is to putt one of the balls into the other. Try to hit the ball as many times in a row as you can. Each time you hit the ball it will move. Do not replace it. Always start from the same location. If you bump the ball with good speed, it will not move too far. The farther the ball keeps getting bumped, the harder the game becomes.

▶ **Down-the-line drill.** Find a level area of the green. Use a chalk line or a suspended piece of twine to create a straight line. Putt the ball and have it remain on or under the line as far as possible. The object is to consistently have it remain on the line a number of times in a row.

▶ **Doorjamb drill.** In a doorjamb, place your head against the wall. Place the ball below your eyes as normal, and make a putting stroke. Keep your head lightly pressed against the wall, and make sure that you do not move your head. If your head moves, it will indicate movement from somewhere else in the body. Figure out what moved, and keep doing the drill until the body becomes movement-free.

9.5. When you get good at putting between the tees, you should be confident in your skill of controlling straight.

▶ **Legs-out drill.** By keeping the legs from moving, you will have a better chance of keeping the entire body from moving. This drill has you focus on keeping your legs still by only using one leg at a time. Address your ball by placing one of your feet opposite the ball with your toes and the knee pointing at the ball. Suspend your other foot in the air behind the planted foot. Make your putting stroke and keep your knee facing the same direction the entire time, without even the slightest bit of wobble. Once you can do it on one foot, switch feet and master the other foot. Once you have mastered both feet individually, putt normally and keep the legs out of the putt.

► **Alignment drill.** Using a mirror, simply take your posture and setup positions as normal, then check in the mirror to see if your alignment is correct. If it is not, move to the correct position. Repeat. Keep repeating until you can correctly align every time, and then repeat some more so you master it and it becomes natural and automatic.

► **Swinging-putter drill.** This drill is to help you focus on what it feels like keeping your arms stable during a putt. Take your putter head in the fingers of one hand, and the butt of the grip in the fingers of the other hand. Hold the putter shaft parallel to the ground with your arms extended straight downward. The drill is simply to rock the putter back and forth without bending or rotating your arms, keeping the shaft on a line parallel to one that would connect your toes.

► **Grip-and-regrip drill.** An essential, yet extremely boring drill is to simply practice taking your grip. I will do this drill while I watch TV, much like pitchers in baseball will repeatedly grip the ball as they would for certain pitches between innings or starts. The idea is that the more often you correctly place your hands onto the putter grip, the more natural a good grip will become, and the more consistently it will work for you. Conversely, it will make it easier to identify when your grip is off. Take your grip, make sure it is correct, let go, and repeat as many times as you can bear it.

► **Rocking drill.** Without a putter, take your arms and crisscross them in front of your chest with your hands on your shoulders. Move your elbows back and forth, keeping them parallel to your toe-to-toe line. This will create the correct rocking motion of the shoulders. (See Figures 9.6 and 9.7.) If you stand in front of a wall while you practice this, your shoulders will remain square to the wall during the motion.

► **Rotation-and-path drill.** Without a putter, extend your fingers and place your palms together. Assume your putting posture and let your arms hang as they would for a putting stroke. Now swing your arms in a putting motion, feeling the inactivity of the hands and wrists. Notice how the hands do not rotate. When this is done cor-

9.6 and **9.7.** This drill is to help you regain the proper feel of rocking the shoulders, especially if the shoulders have been causing pulled or pushed putts.

rectly, your hands will be swinging back and forth on a single path. If you swing your hands over a line on the ground, like a sidewalk crack, you can see how straight the path is.

► **Wall drill.** This is to practice a straight-back straight-through path. Stand facing a wall with your feet parallel to the wall and place the putter so the toe is only about an inch away from the wall. Set up to a ball and make your normal stroke. Your putter should remain the same distance from the wall throughout the stroke.

Training Aids

► **Putt master.** Creating a true pendulum motion will improve your overall putting game dramatically. This aid gives you the ability to feel the exact mechanics of a true pendulum through its unique design. Two cuffs are placed between your wrists, and a metal rod hangs toward the ground, aimed at the putter head. When a good pendulum motion is used to swing the arms, the metal rod will remain pointing at the putter's head throughout the stroke. Use it to eliminate wrist action during your traditional-type stroke.

► **Putting arc.** This training aid is very effective for grooving an inside-square-inside swing path. It has the versatility to be taken with you to the practice putting green or anywhere you practice your putts. It can be made from plastic or wood and is a precision-made single-rail system designed to allow your putter to swing on a precise arcing path. This aid is without doubt the best way to practice your arcing swing path.

► **Putting square system.** As good as the putting arc is for the inside-square-inside swing path, this aid accomplishes the same for the straight-back straight-through path player. This two-rail system is designed to allow you to swing your putter on the perfect straight-back straight-through path. You simply keep your putter head swinging between the rails on both back and forward swings. This aid can be used anywhere but is most effective right on the practice putting green. Using this aid will help you to groove and master the straight-back straight-through swing path.

► **Putting mirror.** To check your alignment positions, as well as your eyes in relation to the ball position, you need an aid that will precisely and consistently provide you with valuable feedback. This device can be used anywhere but is best used at home in the living room. A mirror that has specific markings to aid in the alignment of the putter's face and body, this device is about a foot in length and is placed onto the ground. It has a special dimple built in to allow a golf ball to be used so you can practice your setup with your eyes directly over the ball. Simply use the aid to train your muscles how it feels to be in a proper square setup position. With your eyes properly aligned over the ball position, you will also learn the feel of proper posture.

► **Laser putting alignment system.** This aid is the most effective way to check your putter face's position at setup and your aim. It is a laser device that is attached to your putter; when activated, the laser will point in the exact direction the putter's face is heading. The face needs to be square to your target for success; once the putter's face is aimed, the laser device will give you the undeniable truth as to just how well you have aimed.

► **Sweet spot clips.** To check whether or not you are striking the sweet spot, there is no better tool than a sweet spot clip. This device attaches to your putter's face and has raised rails on either side of the putter's sweet spot, allowing just enough room for you to strike the ball correctly. This gives you instant feedback by sending the ball in the complete wrong direction when you miss the sweet spot. By practicing with this aid, you will train your body to be much more precise and controlled, which will result in better sweet spot hits and more putts holed.

► **Pin balls.** This is a device of two connected golf balls that create a single, double-ball training aid. It is used to determine whether or not your putter face is square at impact. If the balls roll straight, everything is fine. If they spin one way or the other, they tell you exactly the position of your clubface at impact. (See Figure 9.8.)

► **Chalk line.** This is like a tape measure loaded with chalk-coated twine. Simply pull out a desired length and snap it against the green (you might need some help if you're covering a great distance), and you'll have no problem seeing the straight target line.

9.8. This manufactured aid is easier to use than the two separate balls from the square putter face test.

STEP 3: PRACTICE YOUR DISTANCE CONTROL

By now you should have confidence in your mechanics and direction-control skills. It is now time to practice your distance control. Many great drills and training aids focus on distance control. Pick one or more from the following list to effectively practice with. Once you feel good about your distance control, you will be ready to move to step 4 and put all of your skills into practice.

Drills

▶ **Ladder drill.** Take three or four of your irons and place them on the green in a line, end to end but separated by a club length. The object is to putt your ball and have it stop within the length of each iron. Start with the closest iron, which will be about a three-foot putt, then the next, about a nine-foot putt, and so on, adding about six feet for each successive iron. When you reach the farthest iron with success, work your way back to the closest. See how many times you can go through all of the irons without a miss. If you miss, start over with the closest iron. Over time, add more irons, or start with the irons farthest from you. (See Figure 9.9.)

▶ **Setback drill.** This is a drill to use on the practice green. Each hole is a par 2. You putt to a hole. If you make it, you score a birdie. If you miss, regardless of the distance (one inch or six feet), you must move your ball back one club length away from the spot your ball came to rest, directly in line but away from the hole, and then putt from there. See how well you do against par for eighteen holes. You will learn quickly to get your first putt really close to the hole, as well as the importance of three- and four-foot putts.

9.9. You can start with short to long, go long to short, or do both.

► **Semicircle drill.** Pick a hole and place tees one club length away from it, forming a semicircle around the back side of the hole. Choose a distance; start with ten feet, facing the hole. Putt ten balls. Success is either a hole out or a ball that stops within the semicircle. The object is to have all ten balls remain in the semicircle. When ten is achieved, move back five feet and work on that distance. If at any time a ball is unsuccessful you must start over. (See Figure 9.10.) This is a great drill to learn to always get your ball to the hole, while at the same time assuring it does not go flying too far past.

► **Past-the-hole drill.** For the player who seems to always come up short of the hole, this drill is for you. Take ten balls from any distance you choose. I like to start at ten feet. Putt your first ball past the hole, anywhere from two inches to twenty feet, as long as it's past the hole. Putt the second ball past the hole, this time making sure it is past the hole but not as far past as the first. Follow the same procedure for the third ball, but not as far past as the second. Putt all ten balls, each one not as far past the hole as the one just previous. When you master this drill, you will be able to putt the first ball ten ball widths past the hole, the second ball nine ball widths, and so on. If at any time your ball comes up short of the hole, simply start over.

► **Pendulum drill.** With the correct shoulder motion, you will want to create a good pendulum swing to control distance. Each pendulum length will have the ball travel a different distance, so practicing different pendulum lengths is important. For whatever pendulum length you wish to practice, you will set up two balls a particular distance apart. For our example of a three-foot putt pendulum, we will set up the two balls six inches apart plus the width of your putter. Address

9.10. If you miss at any time, you must start over at one.

the putter equidistant between the balls, and simply practice-swing the putter with a consistent pace back and forth between the balls without hitting them. The smoother and more rhythmic your motion becomes, the closer to each ball you can stroke without moving the ball. This practice drill will help you to master your pendulum motion.

► **Rhythm drill.** This drill is designed to help you use your pendulum motion with rhythm. With your putter and a ball, align yourself to make a putt. Stand more upright than normal so the putter is suspended half an inch above the ball. Make a series of pendulum swings above the ball to the length of pendulum that you wish to practice—for example, six inches back and forth. After six continuous pendulum swings, make your seventh strike the ball by lowering your posture to the proper position. You want all seven swings to have the same rhythm.

► **Circle drill.** Place eight golf balls around the hole, starting with the first one about a foot away from the target. Lay each of the remaining seven balls about a foot farther back from the previous one, creating a spiral pattern. Try to make all eight shots without a miss. If you miss, relay the balls and start over. You can start with the close one first or the farthest one first, your choice.

Training Aids

► **Metronome.** Trying to master your tempo without an aid is very difficult. There are digital metronomes that are programmable and can be used anywhere. Practicing to a metronome that can be set up to your particular rhythm is the best way to groove a tempo. With a good tempo, your distance control will be greatly improved.

► **Yardstick.** Use a yardstick to help you gauge the distance of your back stroke and follow-through. Distance control is gained by controlling the length of your motion. Learn how far back you swing to create a particular distance.

► **Whippy Tempomaster.** Another great aid in working on your tempo, this putter has an extremely flexible shaft. You must swing with a smooth tempo to allow the whippy shaft to stay in control and help you to master a repeatable pendulum motion.

STEP 4: PUT IT ALL TOGETHER

You have practiced and drilled your direction and distance skills. You have also made sure that your stroke and mechanics are working properly. The final step in your practice routine should include an activity that incorporates everything into a playing situation while challenging your mental skills as well. Basically, you want this part of the practice to be a game. In other sports, this part of the practice would be called a scrimmage. The scrimmage was always my favorite part of any sports practice. Our golf scrimmage can be played by ourselves or with others, all depending on your preferences and the availability of playing partners. The following is a list of great golf putting games to play as practice that will incorporate all of your putting skills.

Drills

► **Par-2 game.** On a practice putting green, play nine or eighteen holes. Each hole is a par 2. Holes in one are birdies, threes are bogeys, fours are double bogeys, and so on. Play your number of holes and keep your score. Each time you play, try to beat your best score. This is a great game to play by yourself or with however many other players you want to invite.

► **Putting-green match play.** With a partner, play a match. The player with the honors selects a hole and putts first. The player with the lowest score on the hole wins the hole. The winner of a hole always selects which hole to play to next. For ties, the player with the previous honors selects the next hole. Play a predetermined number of holes, for a specific time period, or until one player wins a certain number of holes—your choice.

► **Match-play setback.** Play a match against someone, and every time a ball misses the hole, it must be set one putter length away from the spot your ball came to rest directly away from the hole. In match play, use the longer of the two competitors' putters as the measuring club.

► **Target practice.** If you like the game of darts, this game is for you. Using tees and twine, create a "circle" around a hole (the circle will be more like a spider's web). Wrap the twine around a tee and push the tee into the ground securely holding the twine. Continue around the hole at a radius of about a foot. Now make a second circle the same way, only this one should be about two feet farther out than the first. Do the same for a third, about two feet farther than the second, ultimately creating a bull's-eye target pattern. Hole out for ten points, center circle is five points, the middle circle is three, and the outermost ring is one. All players make ten putts and the player with the most points wins.

► **To-the-line drill.** This is a fun drill that can be played anywhere (for example, putting green, sidewalk, living room). A straight line is drawn or a crack is found, and two players stand at equal distances on opposite sides of the line or crack. Each player putts, and the closest to the line wins a point. Once a player gets to five points, players switch sides. The first to ten points wins.

► **Putting horse.** Randomly choose the honors. The first player gets to choose to putt from anywhere on the green. If the putt is holed, the next person putts and has to make it from the same spot, as will each participating player until someone misses. Once a player misses the putt, the next player in line chooses a new location from which to putt. Only one player will earn a letter following a holed putt. Every missed putt that follows a holed putt earns a letter: an *H* for the first missed putt, an *O* for the second, an *R* for the third, then an *S*, and finally an E. When a person earns all five letters, he or she is out of the game. The last player with letters to earn is the winner.

► **Twenty-one putt points.** Randomly choose the honors. The first player gets to choose to putt from anywhere on the green at least forty feet from the hole. All players putt and points are given as follows: One point for the closest to the hole and the closest to the hole also earns an automatic concession for that hole. Ten points for first holing the putt. Fifteen points for the second player holing the putt. If one of the players three-putts, everyone else gets three points. If a second player three-putts, those players who have not three-putted each get six points. The first player to twenty-one points wins.

Training Aids

► **Golf cup reducer.** By using a golf cup reducer, you make the size of the hole smaller than it is supposed to be. This aid is a plastic hoop that fits perfectly into a regulation-size golf hole, thereby making the hole smaller. Practicing your stroke and playing games with a smaller hole will help your stroke to become more refined and your focus improved. A nice side effect to this aid is that when you take your game to the course, the holes will be much larger than what you have been practicing with. Your confidence will improve after being able to hole out consistently with a tiny golf hole.

► **Artificial putting surface.** These are great if you can afford the expense and the space. There are mats made of a synthetic plastic material to resemble short putting green grass. There are carpets, also made from synthetics, that you would install that will look and play like a real putting green. You can create a putting surface with the exact speeds of the greens at courses where you normally play, as well as adding some breaking terrain. This gives you the ability to practice more often because of the convenience of being at home.

► **Dixx-infinics Computer Putter.** This could be my all-time favorite putting aid. It is a tiny computer, about the size of a cell phone,

9.11. I believe this is just the start of how well technology can assist us in improving our putting.

attached to the putter. It gives you instant feedback on many variables of the putting stroke. It shows how well you level the putter at address, whether or not your hands are steady, the exact swing path you made during the stroke, the impact position on the putter face, open or closed putter face position at impact, and the tempo and speed of the stroke. It keeps track of your practice to give you statistics on how well you fared with each of the variables. It even gives you a "Nice Putt" if you nail all of the variables at once. It is easy to use, gives instant feedback, and is just so cool that it almost makes the other training aids seem a bit old-fashioned. (See Figure 9.11.)

chapter

10

QUESTION-AND-ANSWER TIME

Questions to me are an integral part of a good golf lesson. When I had questions about putters, I found an expert to help me answer them in Bobby Grace, whose interview from Chapter 7 helped me to learn even more about the importance of a good putter. When people come to me for help with their golf game, it is imperative that I encourage them to ask questions. If I spend a lesson doing all the talking, I will have no idea if I am actually giving new or helpful information to the student. Questions give me a feel for a player's level of knowledge, and they enable me to more effectively pass on knowledge that will improve the player's game. Some players have posed questions that have challenged my way of thinking about the game and have led to an improvement in my teaching techniques. The following are important questions I have been asked, with answers that I feel will benefit all players and may even help improve your putting game.

Does the ball matter in putting?

Yes, it does matter. Have you ever tried to putt an egg? If the ball is not balanced or perfectly round, then it cannot roll in a straight line.

A perfectly balanced golf ball will roll in a more consistent line than a ball out of balance. If you ever want to experience the torture of putting with a completely unbalanced ball to prove to yourself the necessity of balance in a ball, buy yourself the trick ball called the Wobbler. It normally is a gag gift built on the premise of an unbalanced golf ball, and how funny it is to see someone unknowingly putt with it. The trick ball is quite obvious in its unbalance, and will almost turn a full circle when struck. A normal golf ball slightly out of balance will hardly seem like it is wobbling off the intended line at all.

Remember, though, that the hole is only three and a quarter inches wide, and any minor wobble will be the difference from a hole out and a lip out miss. Selecting a ball for its balance will only take a little research and some follow-up on your part. First research the golf ball manufacturer's claims. The quality companies will claim that a certain percentage of all of their balls are balanced. For instance, Callaway claims ten of twelve balls to be perfectly balanced. Titleist PV1 claims eleven of twelve. Wilson True claims that twelve of twelve balls are perfectly balanced. You can count on the company's claims, but what that usually means is one or two in each dozen are not balanced.

The next step is to check the balls for yourself. Use the following recipe to find balanced golf balls. Add three or four tablespoons of salt to one cup of water. Mix. Drop the ball into the mixture, and let the ball settle. Use a marker to mark the top part of the ball sticking out of the water. Take the ball out, and then drop it back into the water. If the ball is out of balance, the part that sticks out of the water will again be the part that you marked before. If the ball is balanced, the part that was marked will be in a different location. (See Figure 10.1.) If a homegrown recipe is not your cup of tea, there is a product on the market designed to determine a ball's balance. It is called Check-Go Golf Ball Sweet Spot Finder.

10.1. You can use these homegrown tools to test for a golf ball's balance.

Can I use the same putter for putting on northern and southern greens?

You most certainly can. However, if you play on grainy Bermuda grass in the South and faster bent greens in the North, there may be an advantage to using two different putters. Slower, grainy Bermuda greens can see benefits from a heavier and somewhat more lofted putter, where faster bent grass greens might gain benefits from a bit lighter putter with less loft. I have seen players buy two of the same putters and then have them modified for each location. Some players will even modify a single putter by adding lead tape. Some players simply use the same putter in both locations and alter their mechanics slightly and practice to get the feel of the different green.

Am I stuck with the yips forever?

No. The yips are considered a kind of flinching motion made with the hands during the stroke of a putt. There is some science behind the yips, which are generally a disorder realized by players in midlife or older. Most of the time, the yips occur on short putts, three or four feet and closer. A lot of the time, they do not occur in practice but show up only under competitive circumstances. There really is not a cure for the clinical version of the yips, as far as I am aware, but certain methods can alleviate the problem to some degree, including many that are psychological in nature and involve various imagery and breathing techniques, along with the setting of goals and relaxation strategies.

There are also techniques that involve switching the type of stroke you use. By changing to a stroke that eliminates the need for the hands and wrists, you can bypass the yips. Maybe this is as good as a cure. Any player cursed with the yips needs to attempt whatever technique is possible to help regain putting confidence and the fun of the game of golf again. Professional assistance is always recommended for someone attacked by this affliction.

At what point should I change my putter's grip?

As there is no violent motion required with a putter, the grip does not need to act as a sticky gripping agent to keep the putter from slipping out of your hands. The grip of a putter is there to provide a solid base to hold and to help you feel the stroke. If you have great feel with the old grip you are using and you are making putts, then there is no need to change. If your putting is lacking, then maybe you need to change to a new type of grip. If the grip is falling apart, then I highly recommend changing it. Just find the same exact grip, only new.

Is practicing on my carpet at home beneficial at all?

Practice anywhere is beneficial, as long as you are able to work on your skills improvement. The texture of your carpet will dictate the type of practice you are able to perform. If it is shag carpet, then putting might not be feasible. If it is a tighter weave and matches the speed of your course greens, then put a hole in the floor (or a marker to serve as a target) and practice all day. If the speed of the carpet is different than what you play, just practice your direction-control skill of three feet.

Is there any way to know if any of my thirty putters actually fit me?

The best way to learn if any of your putters will actually fit you properly is to first get a proper fitting customized for you and your stroke, so you know which variables you need. Once you know the variables, you can have your putters checked to see which ones match. If one of your putters comes close, then perhaps a simple alteration will change the incorrect variables to create the perfect putter for your stroke.

Is it better to practice alone or with a friend?

This is solely at your discretion. Some players practice better alone, while others need the competition of a friend. If you are going to be a great putter, you will be doing both. Alone practice time allows you to be more in tune with your thoughts and sensations and to focus on improvement. Practice with friends allows you to challenge your skills in nonstressful competition.

Should I consider a practice schedule?

To create consistency in the putting game, routines are a necessity. A practice schedule is a method of creating consistency. Every player comes with different time restraints and goals, so almost every schedule needs to be customized. I recommend that every player set his or her putting goals and then routinely schedule practice time to accomplish these goals.

Do I really need to worry about putting if I can't control my long game?

I have a lot of players say that there is no need to focus on putting until they have control of their full swing. Playing the game of golf is about scoring as few strokes as possible. Putting will be the greatest stroke saver, and due to the relative simplicity of its mechanics as compared to the full swing, putting will be an easier stroke to learn and make effective. Also, the concepts of putting, as well as a lot of the mechanics, are at the core of creating the full swing. Learn to putt well, and you could actually improve the rest of your game, not to mention lower your score.

Is green reading art or science?

Some people claim that reading a green well is a science, while others claim that it is an art. Which do you think it is? Before I give you my answer, I will explain the two, which will hopefully give you some time to formulate your own opinion, if you haven't already. The art of reading a green may as well be described like any other creative process. Each great green reader possesses his or her own style of green reading. Some players circle the green, reading all the while, and then move behind the ball to finalize the read. Other players start behind the ball, gaining initial insight, and then move around the green looking for more details. Some read the green from behind the ball only. Others read from behind the ball, with a double-check on the opposite side of the hole. There are those who crouch low, some who use the putter as a plumb bob, others stalk, and still others move about with an unknown purpose. Each and every one of them, though, has an understanding of the science involved and has developed over time the ability to visualize how that science affects a rolling ball. The science of green reading is actually many different disciplines combined: physics, meteorology, agronomy, and optics, with physics being overwhelmingly the most important. The art of green reading is using experience, instinct, and feel to determine the proper path. I believe the best green readers are those who have a great understanding of the sciences involved in putting and who then use that knowledge as a tool to allow their minds to artfully visualize the most probable path the ball will have to follow in order to end up in the bottom of the hole. It takes science used as an art to read a green effectively.

Does it matter which of my eyes is most dominant?

It does matter. We all have one eye that is dominant and handles most of our focus. It matters that our alignment is determined by what our dominant eye is seeing. If the dominant eye is not in the correct position, then it will guide you into an incorrect alignment and aim. You might think you have aimed correctly, but your eye has deceived you. You need to know which eye is dominant and then learn to position yourself accordingly. Whichever eye it is, it needs to be positioned directly above the ball with both eyes level to give you the most accurate, nondistorted visual of the intended line. To find out which eye is dominant, extend both arms out with thumbs up. Locate a target in the distance between the thumbs. Close your right eye. If the target remains between the thumbs, then you are right-eye dominant. If the target moves out of the thumbs, you are left-eye dominant. Try this several times, just to make sure it is correct.

What is the secret of putting?

If you asked this to a hundred pros, you would most likely get a hundred different responses, because putting is such an individual experience and every player has his or her own way of stroking the ball. Great putters have learned how to get the ball into the hole by any means possible. One pro's secret may be in how the grip is held. Another pro may be standing in a tall posture, while the next might benefit from crouching. The secret of putting is learning that there is no one magical tip and that there is a unique stroke for every player. Hopefully, after reading this book, you'll not only understand that the only true way to master putting is to methodically determine what works for you, but you'll also have the tools to be successful with your findings.

INDEX

Page numbers in **bold** refer to illustrations.